The Writer's Guide to
Research

The Writer's Guide to
Research

*An invaluable guide to gathering
material for features, novels and
non-fiction books*

MARION FIELD
2nd edition

How To Books

Published by How To Books Ltd,
3 Newtec Place, Magdalen Road,
Oxford OX4 1RE. United Kingdom.
Tel: (01865) 793806. Fax: (01865) 248780.
email: info@howtobooks.co.uk
http://www.howtobooks.co.uk

Second edition 2000

British Library Cataloguing in Publication Data.
A catalogue record for this book is available from
the British Library.

Edited by Diana Brueton
Cover design by Shireen Nathoo Design
Cover image by PhotoDisc
Cover copy by Sallyann Sheridan
Cartoons by Mike Flanagan

Produced for How To Books by Deer Park Productions
Typeset by PDQ Typesetting, Newcastle-under-Lyme, Staffs.
Printed and bound by Cromwell Press, Trowbridge, Wiltshire

NOTE: The material contained in this book is set out in good
faith for general guidance and no liability can be accepted
for loss or expense incurred as a result of relying in particular
circumstances on statements made in the book. Laws and
regulations are complex and liable to change, and readers should
check the current position with the relevant authorities before
making personal arrangements.

Contents

List of Illustrations

Preface
to the 2nd Edition

All writers at some time need to do research. This book explains how to go about it. Whether you are researching for an article, a biography, a textbook or a novel you will find useful information in the following pages. You are shown how to prepare your topic and plan your research. Various research techniques are introduced to you and you are shown how to make best use of them.

Step by step you are given practical information on getting the most from your local library, using the British Library, finding relevant information from the archives and even coping with modern technology and the internet. If you have felt bemused by the thought of researching, this book will show you how to start.

There are sections on interviewing people and preparing and using questionnaires. There is even information on taking part in a sixteenth-century historical re-creation. Sections on costume, transport, manners and language will help you to make your work authentic. In this new edition there is also a chapter on the internet.

Case studies take you through the stages of research used by an article writer, an historian and a novelist. These will help you to see how to put your research to practical use and will show you the finished product. Written in an easy-to-follow style, the book contains plenty of illustrations and you will have no difficulty in selecting the sections that will help you in your research.

The article 'Shere Delight' in Chapter 11 is reprinted with the kind permission of Theo Spring, Editor of *Surrey County Magazine*.

I should like to thank the following for their help with the new Chapter 3:

Vernon White from the Woking Library who helped me to explore the internet.

Susanne Weber who provided information about some useful web sites.

Alistair Etheridge who checked the chapter to make sure it was accurate.

Marion Field

1

Preparing Your Topic

BUILDING UP YOUR RESEARCH LIBRARY

If you are going to be a serious writer, whether of fiction or non-fiction, you will need to do some research. There are certain books that are indispensable for a writer. Some of them you will probably already have. It's a good idea to invest in those you don't possess. It will save you time in the future.

Using the dictionary

Make sure you have an up-to-date dictionary. Remember that a dictionary not only tells you the definition of a word. It also states the part of speech it is. You may be surprised to discover how many words can be used as both **nouns** and **verbs** or **adjectives** and **verbs**. Many words, of course, have several meanings and our language is a very rich one so widen your vocabulary as much as you can.

A dictionary will often give the origin of a word. It is fascinating to browse through and discover from how many languages English is derived.

Making use of the thesaurus

A thesaurus is a *very* useful tool. It will suggest **synonyms** (words that are similar) that can replace overworked words. Frequent use of this will definitely widen your vocabulary.

Dipping into an encyclopaedia

It is very useful to have a general encyclopaedia to which you can refer. Of course, if you are lucky enough to have the complete set of the *Encyclopaedia Britannica*, you will save yourself a number of trips to the library. Encyclopaedias are frequently updated but even older editions are useful as facts and dates don't alter and you can always use the library editions if yours doesn't have the latest information.

Checking your English

Make sure your English is always correct and cannot be faulted. This is essential. There are several guides to good English but *The New Fowler's Modern English Usage* is the standard one. The third edition has been edited by R. W. Burchfield and it is published by Oxford University Press.

Spanning the globe

An up-to-date world atlas is useful. The *Times Comprehensive Atlas of the World* is probably the best and this is updated regularly. Make sure you always check your geographical facts. If you make a mistake, your readers will be sure to point it out.

Looking at England

Another good investment is an up-to-date road atlas of the British Isles. You never know when you might need to check the whereabouts of a town or river. The *AA Big Road Atlas* is updated regularly and this is a good buy. A *London A to Z* street atlas is also useful.

Browsing through guides to writers' markets

The *Writers' and Artists' Year Book*, published by A. & C. Black, is the writer's 'bible'. It should be on the bookshelves of all aspiring writers. It lists most UK and overseas newspapers and magazines. It has a list of UK and overseas publishers. It also provides information for artists, photographers and those who wish to work in radio or television.

As well as the basic information, there are also helpful articles and general information of interest to writers, artists and those who work in all areas of the media. It is updated every year but it is not necessary to replace it every year; most of the information will be the same. However, it should be replaced after a few years as editors and addresses do change.

The Writer's Handbook published by Macmillan also has a wealth of information. This gives more details about prospective markets.

Acquiring press cuttings

Do watch for interesting stories or features in the press. Cut them out and keep a file of cuttings. Organise them in an appropriate order so you can always find what you are looking for. You may have to have a periodic 'blitz' on your cuttings.

Choosing your own research books

Depending on your own speciality, you will, of course, acquire a collection of appropriate books. If you write feature articles or short stories, there are a number of books on the writing of those that would be of interest. There are also books on writing a novel, preparing a synopsis and a host of other titles.

Whether or not you write biography, a biographical encyclopaedia is a great asset. So is a dictionary of dates and a chronological list of historical events.

Checklist of useful books to acquire

- dictionary

- thesaurus

- encyclopaedia

- *The New Fowler's Modern English Usage*

- world atlas

- road atlas of the British Isles

- *London A to Z* street atlas

- biographical dictionary.

DECIDING ON YOUR TOPIC

So you have lots of ideas buzzing around in your brain. Have you noted them down in the notebook you always carry around with you? You may be able to use some of them at a future date. You only need one to work on at the moment.

Researching your market

One of the most important things to do before planning your work is to research the market. It is very important to send editors the type of work their magazines or publishing houses take.

Planning for an article

Before starting work on your article, browse around your local newsagents and note the magazines you are interested in. The library will also have a selection you can study. Buy one or two that use the sort of material you want to write and study those in more detail. Note the length of sentences and paragraphs. How do they set out dialogue? What length do they prefer?

Study the style of the particular magazine you want to write for. Some magazines produce guidelines for writers and these can be very helpful. If you have an idea, submit a query letter to the magazine before starting work on it. The editor may not be interested in the idea so you will have saved yourself some time. Try another magazine but remember to gear your article to it. You can send the same query letter to different magazines. If more than one accepts the idea, your article can be written in a different way or with a different slant.

Planning for a short story
Most women's magazines use a number of short stories. Again you need to read several stories from each magazine so you are familiar with the style and the length.

Planning for a biography
If your chosen genre is historical biography, you should check to see when a biography of your subject was last written. If you have chosen a contemporary subject who has an interesting story, browse round the bookshops to see which publishers have published similar works and write some query letters to them.

Planning for a novel
The complete manuscript of a novel should be sent to your chosen publisher. However, it is better to write a query letter before sending it, in case they are not interested in your particular story. Do read as much modern fiction as possible to see what publishers are currently looking for. Fashions in fiction change rapidly.

Choosing your genre
Have you decided on the type of work you are going to do? If you are writing a book, there is no reason why you cannot use the material you have researched for articles as well. There is plenty of scope.

Focusing your research
By now you will have decided on the period, setting and time span of your work. Don't deal with too large a topic or you will get carried away and your research will take up so much time, you'll never write the book or article. Decide on the time span and the particular aspects of the topic you want to concentrate on.

Revising the points

- Research your market.

- Send a query letter before writing a factual piece.

- Plan your research.

- Don't make your topic too broad.

BREAKING DOWN YOUR TOPIC

Whatever you have chosen and whatever period and time span you choose, it is essential to break your topic down into manageable sections.

Planning your time

Use your time wisely. Don't fritter it away by trying to do too much at once. You will probably end up achieving nothing. Decide what you need to research in a particular place and spend a day or half a day in that library or visiting that museum.

Using headings

Divide your topic into small sections and give each a heading. When you have done that, break each heading down into even smaller sections. Make sure each one is clear and you know exactly what you need to research.

Asking questions

There are six questions that you can ask yourself at the early planning stage:

- **Why** should I write this?

- **When** does it take place?

- **Where** does it take place?

- **Who** is involved?

- **What** happens?

- **How** does it happen?

Revising the points

- Plan your time carefully.

- Don't do too much at once.
- Break down the topic into small sections.
- Ask yourself, 'Why? When? Where? Who? What? How?'

MAKING YOUR RESEARCH STATEMENT

Look back at the questions you have just asked and study your answers.

Raiding your bookshelves
Before starting on your project, look at your own bookshelves and see what material you already have in your possession. Are your books carefully organised so you know exactly where to find certain information? If not, do spend some timing bringing order to your bookcase. It will save you time later.

Making a list
Now make a list of all the facts you need to check and beside them note down where you think you can find the information.

Writing the research statement
It will help you if you can write down briefly what your article or book is to be about. Go to the heart of the matter. To make it interesting there will, of course, be some 'embroidery' to illustrate your points but this does not need to be included in the statement.

Example of an article research statement
Hannah Snell was an eighteenth-century woman who dressed as a man and ran away to sea. Visit the library to research her history. Visit her haunts. What happened to her? Was she unmasked?

WRITING YOUR TOPIC SENTENCE

It is always helpful to encapsulate your article or book into a single sentence.

Focusing your mind
This one sentence will focus your mind on the aim of your writing and will prevent you being waylaid by too many red herrings.

Example of a topic sentence
Trace Hannah Snell's extraordinary career as a sailor in the eighteenth century.

Revising the points

- Check your bookshelves for appropriate material.

- Make a list of what you need to research.

- Write your research statement.

- Write your topic sentence.

PLANNING YOUR RESEARCH OUTLINE

This must be fairly detailed and it will incorporate the outline of the piece you are going to write with the research you need to do. It will be an elaboration of your research statement.

Organising your research

Look at the outline you have done and link together the research you need to do in the library. Make a note of everything you wish to find out. Perhaps you will need to spend more than one day there. Don't forget to take a supply of notebooks and pens.

Will you have to visit other places? Plan your visits so you can fit in as much as possible in the time you have available. Make a trip to a nearby museum while you are in the area. It may have some useful information.

Using your time wisely

By planning your research outline carefully, you will save time and be able to work in a systematic way. This organisation should help you when you come to write your piece.

Revising the points

- Organise your research into sections.

- Do everything in the same place on the same day.

- Plan your time carefully.

CASE STUDIES

Throughout the book we shall be following the experiences of three writers. Here is an introduction to them.

Introducing Esther

Esther is 42. She is a freelance writer who has been successfully published for a number of years. She writes feature articles for a variety of magazines. However, she always writes a query letter to the magazine before starting the article. If the editor is interested, she will submit the article 'on speculation', and it is usually accepted.

As a result of a query letter, she has been commissioned to write an article on the historic village of Shere in Surrey for *Surrey County Magazine*. She spends some time writing her research statement and topic sentence. Then she writes her research outline.

Research outline

- Visit library to research history of Shere. Start with the origin of the village. Domesday Book or even further back. Describe the structure of the village and its society. Make notes and note down sources and page numbers.

- Describe the village today and identify its particular character- istics. Visit Shere and absorb the atmosphere. Visit the church and museum. Buy any guidebooks.

- Highlight particular characters who have passed through or lived there. Talk to local people and take photographs.

Introducing Andrew

Andrew is 22 and works in a supermarket. His secret ambition is to write a bestseller. He has written a novel set during the Second World War but it has been rejected by several publishers. One suggested he should take more care with his research as some of his facts were incorrect.

He decides to start again. He writes an outline of the book noting where he needs to do some research. He then spends a day in the library checking facts and dates. He also makes a note of places and buildings it would be helpful to visit.

Introducing Molly

Molly is 58 and has written a number of historical novels but she is becoming bored with this. She has recently discovered the diary of an unknown suffragette and decides she would like to write a history of the suffragette movement. She writes down the time span of the work and notes places mentioned in the diary she needs to visit. She makes a note to interview any suffragettes who are still alive. She spends a day in the library researching dates and well-known figures. She leaves with a number of biographies and books on the history of the time.

2

Discovering Research Techniques

FINDING OUT WHAT IS AVAILABLE

Once you have decided what you intend to research it is a good idea to sit down and make a careful list of what is available. This will save you time later.

- What do you have on your own bookshelves that will be useful?
- Look in the *Yellow Pages* for any specialist services that you need to research.
- Phone anyone who might be able to give you information and if necessary, make an appointment to visit.
- Contact your local library to see if they have the information you require.

MAKING USE OF LIBRARIES

Your local library will be a great help but don't restrict yourself to that library only. A variety of other libraries, both specialist and general, await you.

Using your local library

Your local library is one of your most valuable assets. Librarians are always ready and willing to help you. As well as stocking a great wealth of books, they will also search out books for you from other libraries. If a book is out of print, they will do a laser search and you may be able to borrow first editions and valuable old books. These will probably not be issued on your usual ticket. You may have to sign for them.

You may also be able to use archive material although you will not be able to take this out of the library. Back copies of local newspapers and magazines can also be studied. If you are not computer literate, the librarian will also be able to help you search for material on the database. More about this later.

Using other public libraries
Libraries in other towns can also be useful. You don't need a ticket to use the reference material in any public library.

Using the British Library
The British Library keeps copies of all books that are published in the United Kingdom. By law a copy of every book published *has* to be sent there immediately it comes out. This applies to self-published books as well as those by commercial publishers. So the Library has a vast store of research material and if you can't find the book you need anywhere else, you can be sure it will be there.

Obtaining a Reader's Ticket
To study in the British Library you must obtain a Reader's Ticket. There is no fee for it but, except in exceptional cases, you must be over twenty-one. If you are an established writer and have been commissioned to write a book for which you need to do research, you can be issued with one when you arrive at the Reader Admissions Office in the Library. To obtain it, you should take your contract or a letter from your publisher and some form of personal identification:

- credit card
- cheque card
- driving licence
- passport.

You will be asked to fill in a form and your picture will then be taken. This will be attached to your Reader's Ticket.

If you wish to use the library on the same day you obtain your ticket, it is wise to arrive early as the Admissions Office becomes very busy. Books have to be ordered before 16.00 for delivery on that day. Your ticket is valid for five years and can be automatically renewed within a year of that date.

Studying manuscripts
Your Reader's Ticket will also give you access to 80 per cent of the manuscripts held by the British Library. If you need to look at other select manuscripts, you may need a further letter of recommendation.

Opening hours
The British Library is open from: 9.30 – 18.00 Monday to Thursday
9.30 – 16.30 Friday and Saturday.

Using the internet
The British Library has its own web site (*www.bl.uk*) on the internet.
You can browse at your leisure. The catalogues are also on the
internet so you can save yourself time by looking at them before you
visit the library. They can be found at *http://opac97.bl.uk* (There will
be more about the internet in the next chapter.)

Address and phone numbers
The British Library moved in 1998 to new premises and is now
situated next to King's Cross Station. The address is:

St Pancras
96 Euston Road
London
NW1 2DB

Telephone numbers:	Switchboard:	(020) 7412 2700
	Reader Admissions Office:	(020) 7412 7677
	Manuscript Office:	(020) 7412 7513
	Visitors' Services:	(020) 7412 7332

Receiving copyright copies
As well as the British Library, there are five other libraries which are
entitled to receive a free copy of every book published in the United
Kingdom. These are the University Libraries of Oxford, Cambridge
and Trinity College, Dublin, the National Library of Wales in
Aberystwyth and the National Library of Scotland in Edinburgh. If
you live near one of these, it might save you a trip to the British
Library in London.

Using college and university libraries
Writers are welcome to use the facilities in any college or university
library. If you think they might have a book or manuscript you need
for your research, ring up the librarian and make an appointment.
Like your local librarians, they will be most helpful and will find you
the material you need. Old documents will be locked up but they will
be brought out for you and you will be reminded to treat them with
care. You will usually be required to fill in a form stating your
reasons for doing the research.

Using specialist libraries

There are also a number of specialist libraries which will have a variety of books, papers and manuscripts on a particular subject. To find out which library you need to consult, ask your local librarian for the current *Aslib Directory of Information Sources in the United Kingdom*. This is a mine of information as it lists nearly every library in the country and also gives details of each library's specialities, facilities and opening hours. It is regularly updated.

Using museum libraries

Most of the major museums will also have specialist libraries so if you are researching the Second World War, the library at the Imperial War Museum would be one of your first visits. The libraries in the Natural History Museum or the Royal Botanical Gardens at Kew would be more use to you if your interests are closer to nature.

Using cathedral libraries

Many cathedrals also have libraries which can be used by members of the public provided an appointment is made.

Checklist of libraries

- your local library
- other regional libraries
- the British Library
- college/university libraries
- specialist libraries
- museum libraries
- cathedral libraries.

DISCOVERING REFERENCE MATERIAL

Using secondary sources

Secondary sources are books that have been written about your subject for which research has already been done. If they are recent, they can be easily obtained from a bookshop or library. If they are out of print, you may be lucky enough to find what you require in a secondhand bookshop, or your library may be able to locate a copy for you. Encyclopaedias, textbooks and biographical dictionaries are also secondary sources.

Using primary sources

Primary sources are more interesting because they are the actual letters, diaries, menus and other original documents that were used at the time. They are not always easy to read as they are often handwritten and deciphering a seventeenth-century letter requires a great deal of concentration. Sometimes, of course, they have been printed. This makes it simpler to read but handling the actual letter that someone wrote can make you feel closer to your subject if you are writing a biography.

Studying reference books

All libraries will have a reference section which contains encyclopaedias, dictionaries, indexes, lists, telephone directories, maps, local history and material on most subjects. You may not remove any of these books from the library but you may spend all day in the library taking notes.

Do remember to make a note of all your sources including the page numbers. You may wish to refer to them again and it is very irritating to have to search for a reference you had already found.

Browse round the reference section in the library to see what they have to offer you. You may be surprised at the variety. Make a note of what there is as it may be of use to you later. If you can't find something, ask a librarian. They will always help you.

Fishing in secondhand bookshops

Secondhand bookshops can produce treasures. You are welcome to browse in them and you may find a gem. Like libraries, they are organised by subject. You might find a diary written by someone during the period you are researching or perhaps an ancient basic textbook will give you an indication of past educational methods.

It is also worth adding to your own library. Do buy books that you think might be of use in the future. You might find an old book on local customs or unusual festivals. Nothing is ever wasted for the writer. You should never throw anything away. You never know when it might be useful.

Browsing through newspapers

Newspapers are a great source of information. Libraries will have back copies of local papers which are of great help if you are writing a local piece. Remember what you are researching. Don't get carried away by other items that attract your attention. It is a great temptation to do so but you must discipline yourself to concentrate on the work in hand.

Newspaper offices will always keep back copies of their papers. But if you wish to study a particular paper, you must be specific. If possible, state the exact date of the paper you require and the type of material you need. You will probably not know the page number but at least the date will help. If you phone and ask for what you require, they will probably send you a photocopy of the piece.

Studying magazines

Libraries will keep back copies of a variety of magazines and will be happy to let you look at them. You might get ideas for articles or novels from old articles. If you require a particular magazine for research purposes and the library does not have it, contact the head office of the magazine and they will probably be able to help you. Do remember to be as specific as you can.

Trawling databases

Databases are lists of information of all kinds which are stored in electronic form. You can find them on computers at your local library. If you are not computer literate and modern technology fills you with horror, don't despair. Your friendly library assistant will be willing to help you with your search. Don't be afraid to ask for help. Make a list of what you need to know and take notes on how to obtain the information. Next time you may be able to find the material you need by yourself.

Revising the points

- Make a list of what you need to research.
- Identify the visits you need to make.
- Visit libraries and ask for help if required.
- Make careful notes.
- Keep a record of all sources and page numbers.
- Browse through secondhand bookshops.
- Study newspapers and magazines.
- Use databases.

SEARCHING OUT ORIGINAL MATERIAL

If you are doing serious research, at some time you will need to find

and study original documents. These are often valuable and you will
have to obtain permission to look at them. The Department of
Manuscripts at the British Library has already been mentioned.
This contains an index of ten volumes listing all the manuscripts
held in the Library. You may have to look no further.

Discovering what exists
There are several places which hold public records; many documents
are not released for public scrutiny until thirty years later but
records which are available can be studied.

The Public Record Office
Official documents are automatically deposited in the Public Record
Office. It houses documents dating back to the eleventh century. In
1976 most of the records were moved from London to Kew. It is
hoped that eventually all documents, except perhaps census
documents, will be kept at Kew. A reader's pass is necessary if
you wish to look at any documents. The address is Ruskin Avenue,
Kew, Richmond, Surrey TW9 4DU. Tel: (020) 8876 3444.

There are also Public Record Offices in Scotland and Northern
Ireland. In both, reader's tickets are required. The addresses follow:

Scottish Record Office, HM General Register House, Edinburgh
EH1 3YY. Tel: (0131) 556 6585.

Public Record Office of Northern Ireland, 66 Balmoral Avenue,
Belfast BN9 6NY. Tel: (01232) 251318.

General Register Office
Registers of births, marriages and deaths can be found at the
General Register Office, St Catherine's House, 10 Kingsway,
London WC2B 6JP.

You do not need an appointment to go to St Catherine's House.
To find the record of a particular person, you have to consult the
index of the appropriate year. Having found it, you fill in a form
stating your requirement and, for a fee, the certificate you require
will be photocopied and sent to you. Postal and telephone
applications are also acceptable. Tel: (020) 7242 0262.

The National Register of Archives
The National Register of Archives is housed at Quality House, Quality
Court, Chancery Lane, London WC2A 1HP. This consists of
thousands of lists and catalogues of manuscript collections. No

telephone enquiries are accepted but the Search Room is open to the public. It may be better to visit it as only a few enquiries are handled by post. If you do write for help, remember to enclose a stamped addressed envelope. A limited number of fax enquiries are dealt with and if you choose this method, the fax number is (020) 7831 3550.

Searching parish records
Churches will keep parish records which can prove very interesting and useful. There will be registers of baptisms, confirmation and weddings, some of them going back many centuries. Records of fees paid for weddings and funerals will also be kept and the change from the amount charged in past years can be startling. There will also be Minute books of the proceedings of the Parochial Church Council. These, too, can give an insight into the concerns of past ages.

Using cathedral archives
Most cathedrals will have archive collections and these are also available to the public if an appointment is made and a reason given for the quest. Sometimes a reader's ticket is required. Lists of cathedrals which have libraries and archive collections can be found in your local library.

Checklist of archive sources
- Public Record Office
- General Register Office
- parish records in churches
- cathedral archives.

MAKING VISITS

It will often be necessary to visit places and buildings to add to your research. In some cases, you do not need to make an appointment but for others it is advisable.

Visiting museums
Museums will give you a great deal of information about different historical periods and a wide variety of subjects. You can learn about costume, weapons, medicine, food, famous people and many other areas of interest.

National museums
Many of our great national museums are situated in London. There are the British Museum, the Victoria and Albert, the Natural History and the Science Museum to name but a few. Each of them will be divided into sections so when you are doing your research, don't get carried away by all the other interesting things you see. Remember you are there to study your particular area; go straight to that, trying not to be deflected from your path.

Some museums will have costumed models to add to the interest. Occasionally the whole area will be set in a particular period with costumed characters going about their work as they would have done years ago. These museums are a bonus as you can talk to those who are working there. You will find they have studied the period extensively and will be able to answer your questions. Don't forget to take your notebook.

Most museums possess far more material than they can display at one time. If you think they might hold something that would be of use to you, write to the curator and make an appointment explaining what you need. He or she will usually be happy for you to view any items not on display and will probably be able to give you more useful information.

Local museums
Small independent museums specialising in the area you are researching can prove very useful. It is a very good idea to talk to the curators. They are usually very enthusiastic about their museums and more than willing to impart any specialist knowledge they have. Whenever a curator gives you time, don't forget to write a letter of thanks afterwards.

Specialist museums
There are many specialist museums situated around the country and your local library will be able to help you find those that would be useful to you. Identify the area around which you are working and see what it has to offer. County tourist offices are also very willing to send information to you.

Visiting art galleries
Art galleries, too, can be useful. From paintings you can discover costume details, the architecture of the time, how certain things were done and even what type of food was eaten.

The National Portrait Gallery, round the corner from the

National Gallery in Trafalgar Square, can be used extensively in the study of costume, hair style and head-dresses. Not all their paintings will be on show so do ask if they have a portrait of a certain person or portraits from a particular period.

USING AUDIO AND VISUAL MATERIAL

As well as using the written word, pictures and artefacts, there is now a wealth of material on film, tape and disc. Researchers in the future may use these resources even more than the written word.

Watching films and videos

Television companies are always willing to hire out videos of documentaries and old films. There are documentaries on a variety of subjects. Watching these on video can be very useful as you can stop the video whenever you need to and re-run it to check the details. You can take notes while viewing and go back if you miss something. There are documentaries on a variety of subjects. Programmes produced for the Open University and schools programmes might also be useful. The addresses for the BBC and ITV companies are in the *Radio Times*.

For other film information try the British Film Institute Library, 21 Stephen Street, London W1P 1PL. Tel: (020) 7255 1444. You can take out a library membership for about £25 or a one day reader's pass for £5.00

The old Pathé News Reels give contemporary pictures of news events – particularly during the Second World War – and the British Film Institute may be able to help you track these down.

The Museum of Moving Image on the South Bank in London is well worth a visit. Here you can experience the history of cinema from silent films to the most modern technology.

Accessing the sound archives

The National Sound Archive is housed in the former building of the British Library at 29 Exhibition Road, South Kensington, London SW7 2AS. The BBC sound archives can also be accessed through the National Sound Archive. If you wish to use either facility, it is wise to telephone first. The number is (020) 7589 6603.

Using microfiche
Lists of available radio programmes, drama and other useful

material may be found on microfiche in your local library.

However, you may find that rather than microfiche, the material is stored on databases in the computer. These will usually be found in public libraries.

Discovering oral histories

The oral tradition is far older than radio and film and possibly even than the written word. For centuries folk from different countries, cultures and traditions have told stories and related events which have been passed down the generations. Often these have been greatly embroidered in the process!

Because of the growth of modern technology in parts of the world, this tradition has been in decline, but in recent years there has been a resurgence of interest.

There is now an Oral History Society based in the Department of Sociology, University of Essex, Colchester, Essex CO4 3SQ. Tel: (01206) 873333.

Collecting life stories

In 1993 the National Sound Archive ran a competition entitled 'The National Life Story Collection'. The aim was to collect records of the lives of a variety of people of all ages and from all walks of life.

There were three categories and none of the entries had been previously published.

- **Written category.** This was to be a written life story of up to 70,000 words by an author of 50 or over.

- **Taped category.** The life story of an individual of 50 or over recorded either on audio cassettes or VHS video cassette. The maximum length was three hours. This could be an interview.

- **Young interview.** This was an interview recorded either on audio cassette or VHS video cassette. An individual of 50 or over would be interviewed by a young person of 11 to 16.

The competition was very popular and the material now stored in the National Sound Archive should prove an invaluable source of research in the future.

CASE STUDIES

Esther researches the history of Shere

Having done her research outline, Esther goes to the library because she knows that in the reference section there is a very detailed history of Surrey and its villages written by a nineteenth-century historian. Unfortunately he died before he could finish it, but it was completed by someone else. As it is an old book, it cannot be taken out of the library so Esther spends the day there making notes and always writing the page numbers in the margin so that she will be able to refer to the material again. She discovers that Shere had a link with Edward the Confessor whose wife, 'Eddid, the Queen, did hold it.'

Returning home, she writes a brief outline of Shere from the eleventh century to the present day. Now she has the skeleton of the article, she will have to flesh it out with interesting detail.

Andrew browses in the Imperial War Museum

Andrew is getting very enthusiastic about his book. He is sure it will be so much better than his first attempt.

He spends a day in the Imperial War Museum, disciplining himself to avoid any areas that do not deal with the Second World War. He has taken a notebook and makes copious notes about the type of planes used and the life of the time. He is particularly fascinated by the section dealing with rationing and is amazed at the type of food the British were forced to eat. He takes down some of the recipes as he thinks they might be useful.

Also useful is the re-created underground shelter where he sits with other interested visitors as the air raid warning wails around them. He shudders as bombs drop and the area is shaken. Blinking, he comes out, relieved that the skies above London are now free of enemy aircraft. He acquires a new respect for his grandparents' generation.

Molly works in the British Library and visits *The Times*

Molly is still researching facts. She has acquired a Reader's Ticket for the British Library and has spent a day there, reading and making notes on anything about the suffragette movement she can find. She has become completely absorbed.

She stays in London overnight so that the following day, she can visit the offices of *The Times* newspaper. She has phoned to make an appointment to look at any newspapers that reported the activities of the suffragettes. Later she will also visit the offices of the *Guardian* and the *Daily Telegraph*.

3

Utilising the Internet

The **internet** is a network of computers which are linked around the world by phone lines. It is a portmanteau word created from the two words *inter*national *net*work.

LOOKING AT THE ORIGINS

The idea to connect computers across the United States originated from the US Defense Department in 1969. By 1972 37 computers were connected and in 1984 another US agency, the National Science Foundation, took over the system. Gradually access to the 'internet', as it came to be known, became more widely available.

However, at first it was only large companies that were able to make use of the service. Then some entrepreneurs realised that if certain computers were connected to phone lines, access would be available to anyone who had a phone line.

Explaining the Internet

Today the world wide network of computers can be accessed directly from your PC through the agency of an **Internet Service Provider (ISP)**. There are a number of these companies. They will usually charge you a monthly fee to connect you to the internet but some may be free and only charge you for local calls.

GETTING CONNECTED

To become connected to the internet, you will need three things:

- an appropriate computer
- a modulator-demodulator (modem)
- an internet service provider (ISP).

Assessing your computer

If you wish to use the internet, you may need to buy a new computer. Your old one may be too slow to explore effectively all the data. You should ask for an IBM-compatible PC with a Pentium processor and at least 32 megabytes of Random Access Memory (RAM).

Choosing a modem

A modulator-demodulator (modem) is a device that has to be attached to your computer in order for it to be linked with other computers via a phone line. If you buy a new PC, you will probably find that the modem is already fitted to it. However, if you already have a PC, you should check whether it has a modem and if not you will have to buy one. Modems can be fitted either internally or externally. You are advised to choose an external one. These are available in different designs and should be easy to connect to your PC. One end of the cable is attached to the power supply and the other end to the vacant serial port at the back of your PC. If you are unsure how to do this, seek the advice of an expert. There are plenty of them around!

Finding an internet service provider

Before you can access the Internet, you must sign up with an Internet Service Provider (ISP). This is an organisation which will connect your PC and modem to the Internet via a phone line. There are currently over 200 ISPs in the UK so you will have to shop around to find the one that is best suited to your needs. Some charge a monthly fee which gives you unlimited access while others charge by the hour. There are also a number of companies who provide free access to the internet. These include Freeserve from the Dixons Group, Tesco, Virgin Net and British Telecom. Figure 1 gives a list of some ISPs with their phone numbers.

AOL	0800 376 5432	Free Dot Net	(0180) 938 3338
BT Internet	0800 800 001	Global Internet	0870 909 8041
CIX	(020) 8255 5050	ntl	0800 052 8704
Compuserve	0870 6000 800	Virgin Net	0500 558 800
Freeserve	0906 251 7517		

Fig. 1. List of internet service providers.

Your ISP will provide you with the necessary software to install in your machine.

USING EMAIL

Electronic mail (email) is the most widely used service on the internet. By it you can send and receive messages all over the world. You can even attach documents to your message and you can store your own messages until you are ready to read them. You will have been provided by your ISP with the relevant software.

Sending email
You will find it easy to send an email. Click on the appropriate button, type in the recipient's name and email address and then type in your message. Press the 'send' button and your message is on its way.

Recognising email addresses
All email addresses follow the same pattern. The user's name, company or other identification is followed by @ and the address of their service provider. Here is an example. Julie Smith's Service Provider is CIX.

> *Julie.Smith@cix.co.uk*

Make sure you type it correctly. It will not work if you have left a space or omitted a full stop! Email addresses contain no spaces but a number of 'dots'.

Receiving email
When you connect with the internet, a message on the screen will tell you if you have some email messages and how many. You can then:

- Leave them in your mail box to deal with later.
- Download them (transfer them to your own computer) and read them later.
- Read them now and reply if necessary.

Replying to messages
Replying to your messages is simple. You will probably find a 'reply' button and when you press it, the recipient's address is automatically inserted and you then add your message.

Looking at the advantages

As a writer there are many advantages provided by email.

- You can send letters and ideas to editors quickly.
- Editors will be able to contact you more quickly.
- Completed work can be sent to editors saving on time, postage and stationery.

DISCOVERING THE WORLD WIDE WEB

For research purposes 'surfing the net' in your particular fields will probably be the most important aspect of the Internet for you.

Introducing the web

The **world wide web** contains a vast collection of documents that are stored on computers all over the world. Each **web page** is connected to hyperlinks. The web is part of the Internet and it is invaluable for research.

There is so much material available that at first you may feel completely bewildered but, as you find your way around the web, you will be able to identify the web sites that will be the most use to you.

Using a search engine

Because there is so much information stored on the web, you may have difficulty in finding the web site you require. This is where a search engine can help you. It is like an index to the web and is a tool that will search the Internet for you to find specific references. To activate one for the first time enter its **uniform resource locator (URL)**.

There are a number of search engines which usually require you to type in a keyword and then press 'search'. You can then sit back and wait for the search engine to indicate the sites that might be useful to you. When they appear on your screen, you can access any you wish by clicking on the appropriate hyperlink. One of the most popular search engines is AltaVista. Its URL is *www.altavisa.com*

Finding a web browser

A **web browser** is useful when you know exactly which web sites you wish to visit. It enables you to move from one page to another using hyperlinks. Two of the most popular are Netscape Navigator (*www.home.netscape.com*) and Microsoft Internet Explorer (*www.microsoft.com*)

Bookmarking useful pages

All web sites will have their own addresses. However, if you use particular sites on a regular basis, you can use a **bookmark** to identify these. Add the addresses to your 'address book' where you are able to store them so that you will not need to type in the address every time.

Looking at a web site

A **web site** is a collection of web pages often dealing with a particular subject. Each one is maintained by an organisation or an individual so you may find the information you require located at several web sites. There are a wide variety of web sites so there is a vast amount of material stored on the web.

Finding the home page

The home page is the first page of a web site. It usually gives you an introduction to the site and you will discover the information it offers. When your web browser identifies a site, the home page is the first one you will see.

Surfing the web

Although it is relatively easy to 'surf the web', you may be bewildered at first by the amount of information stored. This is why search engines and web browsers are necessary tools. More web sites are being added all the time.

MAKING THE MOST OF THE NET

As well as using the net for research purposes, you can use it to improve both your writing skills and your chances of being published.

Identifying useful web sites

There are a number of sites that may be of interest to you as a writer.

Correcting your grammar

The most useful grammar web site is The Guide to Grammar and Writing. Based in North America, it is a useful guide although you must remember that there will be some differences in spelling and usage. The sections are divided into sentence work, paragraph work and essay work and it is easy to click on to the particular item you require.

The site contains a very useful Ask Grammar feature which is free and available to anyone wherever they live. Any grammatical questions you ask will be answered within a few days. The URL of this useful site is: *webster.commnet.eduHP/pages/darling/grammar.htm*

Using the dictionary or thesaurus

While your PC will probably contain a dictionary and thesaurus, this may be fairly basic. The web site Research-It (URL *www.itools.com/research-it/research-it.html*) will provide you with a wealth of language information. Among its resources are:

- a dictionary
- computing dictionary
- rhyming dictionary
- thesaurus
- biographical dictionary
- bible dictionary
- dictionary of quotations.

Bookmark Research-It for future reference. It also contains other useful information for writers.

Taking writers' courses

Some established correspondence schools now offer courses over the net. Even if they don't, they are usually happy to receive material by email. There are also a number of courses that are available entirely over the web. Among them is The Friendly Pencil, a US-based course conducting lessons by email and showing course material on its web site.

Meeting other writers

The web provides an excellent place for meeting other writers from all over the world and a means of talking to them.

Finding writers' circles

Many traditional writers' circles now have their own web sites while others are based entirely on the web. Browse around the world and see what you can find. Some send out mailing lists to their members. Others encourage debate through their mailing lists. You have plenty of choice. You might find someone with similar ideas who is willing to pool material or perhaps collaborate with you on a project.

Using a newsgroup
Newsgroups are electronic noticeboards on which anyone can place notices. There are a vast number of them all over the world on every possible subject. By accessing a particular newsgroup you can read its messages, reply to them if you wish and add your own. It is a stimulating way to communicate with other writers.

Looking at sites for fiction writers
The following sites might prove useful if you write fiction:

- *www.purefiction.co.uk/*
- *www.noveladvice.com/previous.htm* A bonus on this site is that you can subscribe to a free email.
- *www.novellearn.com/* A free magazine is available on this site.

Finding Christian writing sites
If you are writing for the Christian market, you might find the following sites useful:

- *www.suite101.com/welcome.cfm/christianwriting*
- *www.ilovejesus.com/lot.epistlewriter.TCWCpage.html*

Searching for quotations
If you are searching for a quotation, you might find the following sites useful:

- *www.cyberquotations.com/quotations.htm*
- *www.motivateus.com/cbt/htm*
- *www.followyourdreams.com/food.html*

MARKETING YOUR WORK

The Internet provides increased opportunities for freelances so don't ignore it.

Checking on-line publishers

Many traditional publishers now have their own web sites. Others, who have recently set up in business, operate entirely on the internet. One of these is Online Originals (*www.onlineoriginals.com*). Another is Haford Publishing (*www.haford.demon.co.uk*) which is prepared to show unpublished novels on its web site. The latter is also willing to negotiate with your publishers the sale of an electronic version of your published book.

Publishing poetry on-line

The Poetry Exchange is a site where poets can publish their poems free of charge. Submitted poems appear very quickly on the site. Many of the poems you can read on London's tube trains are accessible on the Poems of the Underground web site (*www.netpoems.com*)

Creating your own web site

When you sign on with your service provider, you will probably be given some web space to set up your own web site. Anyone can visit it if they have your URL so it is worthwhile investing your time to create your own home page. There are many advantages.

- Your CV can be included.
- You can provide samples of your writing.
- It can help you market your work.
- Your readers can contact you easily.
- Potential clients can get in touch with you.
- You can generate publicity for yourself.

Getting help

There are a number of website designers who, for a reasonable fee, will design and implement your website for you. Brian Jordan of Cobweb Web Design is building up a list of resources for writers on his own website, among them the following:

- on-line publishers
- writers' courses
- help for self-publishers
- small presses.

More resources are frequently being added.

He will also provide a showcase for writers. At no charge he is willing to put samples of your work on the internet. His address is:

57 Moorlands Crescent
Huddersfield HD3 3UF
Tel: (01484) 658881
Web site: *www.kobweb.co.uk*

Promoting yourself

As well as having your own home page, you can also publicise your work on various other sites where you can advertise your services and include examples of your work.

Authorlink (*www.authorlink.com*) is one of these. It provides a wealth of US market information and will show your unpublished article or book on the web site.

Another very useful web site is Subject Books Worldwide (*www.subject-books.co.uk*). This will advertise your books on the internet under subject headings. It also provides a search facility to help you find books and a booksellers' and publishers' directory. Each month it will advertise a Book of the Month. For more information contact:

Derek Pearce
Subject Books Worldwide
Outside Directors Ltd
Reepham
Norfolk NR10 4RP
Tel/fax: (01362) 688588
Email: *dpearce@outside-directorsltd.co.uk*

Researching your markets

You will find a number of other sites which regularly publish market information and these can prove invaluable. Here are three of them:

- Poets-Writers Home Page (*www.pg.org*)
- Market List (*www.marketlist.com*)
- Inklings (*www.inkspot.com/inklings*)

Looking at on-line bookshops

Booksellers are also getting in on the internet act. Amazon is a huge US-based on-line bookseller but it now has a UK subsidiary (*www.amazon.co.uk*). This offers over a million titles and you can browse through catalogues at your leisure.

You can also promote your own books by adding a commentary about them for readers. This can consist of a brief synopsis, a picture of the cover, reviews, blurb and anything else you wish to add.

Some traditional bookshops also have web sites but other UK-based on-line bookshops are:

- Alphabet Street (*www.alphabetstreet.infront.co.uk*)
- The Country Bookstore (*www.countrybookstore.co.uk*)
- The Internet Bookshop (*www.bookshop.co.uk*)
- The Internet Christian Bookshop (*www.icb.nu*)
- Perivale Christian Bookshop (*www.christnetbooks.co.uk*)

COUNTING THE COST

If you are sensible, the cost of using the internet should not be too high. At the end of 1999 the average cost of an ISP was about £10 a month. Some ISPs have a number of discount schemes so you should shop around. You will probably be provided with an off-line mailer which will enable you to store your messages and read them during off-peak hours.

Installing a second telephone line
If you wish to use the internet for research, you won't wish to tie up your telephone line for long periods at a time. Installing a second line will prevent this worry. You will find many ISPs will offer you various discounts so study the options carefully. Using the internet at off-peak hours will, of course, be cheaper but this may not always be possible.

Using Internet cafés
If you are not connected to the world wide web, you can still have access to it through a number of internet cafés. These are cafés which have an area set aside for computers which are linked to the Internet. A half-hour session on one of the computers costs about £2.50. It costs double if you would like an assistant to keep an eye on your progress. It is advisable to book your slot.

If you are totally bemused by all this technology, you can have a training session which will cost about £15 for half an hour. A kindly expert will guide you through the intricacies of the Internet and point you in the right direction for your research.

There is a list of some internet cafés at the back of the book, but to find your local one look in the *Yellow Pages* under internet or restaurants. If you can't find one listed, ask at your local library.

Taking a taster session
The BBC has been instrumental in offering free access to the Net by encouraging taster sessions at various venues across the UK. These include:

- libraries
- adult education centres
- schools
- colleges
- supermarkets
- pubs
- shopping centres.

You will sit in front of a screen wearing earphones and there will be an expert nearby to provide help should you need it. The 'lesson' is carefully planned and you are told exactly what to do. Even if you are not technically inclined, do try it. You may find you enjoy it.

Even if you decide not to install the internet on your computer, you can still use it in the above venues for a small fee. It is here to stay so don't neglect it.

REVISING THE POINTS

- Choose an external modem.
- Find a service provider.
- Find a search engine and web browser to help you surf the internet.
- Create your own web site.
- Use the facilities provided by writers.
- If you are not connected to the internet, use an internet café or try a taster session.
- Don't ignore the internet. It's here to stay.

CASE STUDIES

Andrew surfs the Internet

Andrew is delighted that his parents have finally allowed him to connect his computer to the internet. He spends hours browsing through it but eventually decides that he must focus his surfing. Having found an appropriate search engine, he types in Second World War and is delighted when a number of very useful web sites appear. However, he realises he must narrow down his search. He hopes to visit the Imperial War Museum so he types that in and browses through the information. He notes down particular sections that he feels will be helpful to visit.

Molly visits Cyberia

While Molly is in London, she decides to visit Cyberia, the first
Internet café to be introduced in London. A young man helps her to
'surf' the suffragettes. She is fascinated by the amount of
information that is stored but finds that some of it is not relevant
to the work she is doing. She is not computer literate and feels that
she would rather stay with books! However, she makes some notes
on some of the new information she finds.

4

Using Personal Documents

MAKING USE OF DIARIES AND LETTERS

You can gain a great deal of valuable information from diaries and letters written at the time about which you are writing.

Reading diaries

Diaries are an invaluable source of material. They are written for many different reasons. Some famous people have written with an eye to publication. Others have used a diary as a friend because there was no one else to talk to. In this case there was no thought of publication. Anne Frank's diary is a good example of the latter.

Some people have kept diaries to chart their spiritual progress. Perhaps a journal is a better word for these. Susanna Wesley, the mother of John Wesley, the eighteenth-century preacher and founder of Methodism, kept a journal in which she noted down her thoughts and meditations. During the previous century Samuel Pepys kept a detailed diary of his social life. This provides us with a fascinating insight into life in London after the Restoration of Charles II to the throne.

Reading letters

Letters can also be fascinating. They can shed extra light on a famous event; they can detail a relationship; an acrimonious quarrel can be carried on by letter. Also, of course, they provide interesting material about the time in which they are written.

Getting the feel of the language

If you are writing about an earlier period in history, reading diaries and letters of the time can give you a 'feel' for the language. Although you don't need to write your book or article in the language of years ago, you will need to suggest it. When using dialogue, you will need to check on the form of speech and the language used. In recent times language has become rather sloppy and peppered with new expressions and words. Take care in your writing not to use words or expressions that were not used in the period you are researching. Abbreviations are used much more now than they were in the 1920s and before.

When writing a period piece, try occasionally to use a less modern word in the narrative. This will help to create the right atmosphere.

Making notes on social habits

Diaries can give an insight into how people lived in bygone days as well as helping you to understand a particular person. However, you must be aware that the truth is sometimes embroidered; deliberately or not, diarists do not always tell the absolute truth. Even facts are sometimes incorrect.

You must check your facts with other sources to make sure you are as correct as you can possibly be. The further back in time you go, the more difficult it is to be positive your facts are correct. You will sometimes find that two sources give different dates for the same event.

Make brief notes on anything you read that may be of use and don't forget to identify the source giving the title of the work and the page number. You will then have no difficulty in finding it again. You may not use all the information you acquire but you should always know more about your subject than actually appears in your work.

Quoting from diaries and letters

If you need to use direct quotations from diaries or letters, do make sure you obtain written permission and acknowledge the quotation. Write to the publisher of the diary or letters and ask if you may quote. If the person is still alive or the material is in a private collection, write to ask if you may use it.

Revising the points

- Make notes on anything relevant.
- Don't forget to write down the source and page number.
- Check your facts in more than one source.
- Get permission to quote.

USING AUTOBIOGRAPHIES AND BIOGRAPHIES

Both autobiographies and biographies can be of use in researching a variety of subjects. Details of social life, little known facts about public figures, personal descriptions of public events, costume and other useful information may be gleaned. These may be useful even if the subject of the book is not of primary interest.

Gleaning facts from an autobiography

Autobiographies are particularly important because they provide authentic information about the subject's way of life and often suggest what particular issues were important at the time. Because they are contemporary, they will also be vital for understanding the way in which people thought and spoke and the language used.

Adapting the language

If you are writing an historical novel, be aware of the language used at the time and suggest it in your own work. But don't get carried away and use so many old-fashioned expressions and words that a modern reader will have difficulty in understanding it.

The same would apply to a popular biography. Suggest the appropriate language but don't overdo it.

Writing about real people

If you are writing an historical novel based on real people, you must get your facts right. If not, you will certainly receive irate letters from your readers. However, you will obviously want to embroider the facts so that you can weave a story around them. In this case do state clearly in the frontispiece that this is what you have done.

A biography is different. If the subject is still living or has relatives still alive, you should get permission to do the work. Although it is possible to write an 'unofficial' biography without the blessing of the family, you are unlikely to be very successful without their co-operation. The family may let you have access to private papers that have not been used before. They may even recount anecdotes you can use.

Researching biographies

Biographies can give a different slant to your subject. Don't just read one. Often several biographies about a famous person have been written at different times. One might be written during the subject's lifetime, another just after the death and a third several years later. They will all be different and give you a variety of information. The first one will provide a contemporary view of the subject while the later biographer might have had access to papers denied to earlier biographers.

Revising the points
- Get the feel of the language.

- Occasionally use a less modern word.

- Write appropriate dialogue.

DISCOVERING PRIVATE PAPERS

If your subject is contemporary or there are descendants, approach the family tactfully to ask if any private letters or memoirs of your subject are available. If so, ask for permission to view them, saying you will acknowledge the source in your book.

You may find the family very helpful and you may even unearth a gem that no else has used. Although many papers of some famous people end up in museums, some are still kept by the family so it is certainly worthwhile approaching the relatives.

PAYING ATTENTION TO DETAIL

Detail is very important in whatever form you are writing. It is the well-researched details that give your work authenticity. By reading widely, you will discover incidents and snippets that can be incorporated into your writing.

However, do make sure you are accurate. Check that the costumes worn by your characters are correct for the period. If one of your characters encounters Lady Astor at a meeting in Plymouth, do check she was actually there at the time.

Revising the points
- Try to find private papers.

- Use relevant detail to make your text authentic.

- Check your facts carefully.

UTILISING BUDGETS, ACCOUNTS AND MENUS

You may also find in private collections details of food and other necessities bought.

Looking at hostesses' records

Many hostesses kept detailed accounts of house guests and dinner guests. You might occasionally be lucky enough to discover a visitors' book signed by famous guests. As the date is likely to be included, it is useful to make a note that, for example, Winston Churchill stayed at Cliveden in March 1922.

It was a great honour to entertain royalty and signed photographs of the sovereign grace many stately homes.

Dinner menus were usually displayed on the table and these can often be found in museums or great houses. The variety of courses and the unusual names of some of the items can provide rich pickings for the researcher.

The lady of the house may also have left a record of her own expenditure showing the annual budget allowed her by her husband and the cost of her wardrobe.

Searching through the housekeeper's and butler's records

Housekeepers had to keep detailed records of what they spent and these accounts make interesting reading. The price of goods is worth noting as you may need it in some section of your work.

The butler's records will indicate how much wine was bought and the cost of it. All of this is grist to the researcher's mill.

UNEARTHING LOCAL HISTORY

County historians, town histories and village histories should be studied with care so that you can use the information to make your setting authentic. Nothing can replace visiting the place you are writing about but by studying books about the area, written at various times, you will discover details that you might not find out by visiting.

Finding guidebooks to the area

Many places will have produced guidebooks of their areas highlighting the notable features. The local library will probably store these. You will also find more general books which give information about a wider area. As these do not always contain the same information, do not be satisfied with looking at only one. Study as many as you can find and make notes.

Some areas will have attracted an enthusiastic local historian who has written a detailed account of the county. You may have to search carefully through to find the area you need but it is a worthwhile exercise and you may discover something you didn't know about your area.

Finding out about local events

Very easy to find once you are in the area are booklets detailing unusual events. You might find information about local murders, ghosts, unusual people, strange crimes and local customs. Perhaps there was once a fair held annually. Are there special celebrations on May Day? Does the area still continue to hold events which date back many centuries? You might be able to include the details in your book.

Revising the points

- Make a note of the type of food and the cost.

- Find out as much as you can about the area.

- Buy local guidebooks.

CASE STUDIES

Esther researches Shere's origins

Esther has visited the library again to find out what the Domesday Book recorded about the village of Shere. She discovered that in 1086 when the Domesday Book was compiled, Shere was worth £15 and was 'rated for nine hides'. A 'hide', she learns, was the amount of land considered necessary to support a peasant family for a year. She decides this will make an appropriate opening for her article.

Andrew finds out about life during the Second World War

At the Imperial War Museum Andrew has bought a book on rationing and the food of the time. He finds it very interesting and makes some notes on how his characters coped with rationing. He decides they will buy some food on the black market.

In a secondhand bookshop, he has found two wartime autobiographies. He is delighted to find there is a great deal in each of them about living conditions during the period he is researching. He makes copious notes. He had no idea life had been so difficult.

He writes down unusual incidents that he may be able to use.

Molly sorts out the facts

Molly is spending the week sorting out the information she now has and making notes from the books she has acquired. She puts the information in order and starts to plan her book. She has so much information about individual suffragettes that she decides she must use their stories in the book. She plans to visit some who are still alive and tape interviews with them.

She also writes to a suffragette whose name she has been given. The lady now lives in Scotland so Molly knows she will not be able to interview her. She therefore writes to her for information (see Figure 2).

Dear Mrs Lane

I am a writer and I have been commissioned to write a book on the history of the suffragette movement. I understand that you were involved in it. Would you be able to write down any incidents that you can remember in which you were involved? I would be very grateful if you could help in this way. I enclose a stamped addressed enveloped in the hope that you will reply.

Yours sincerely

Molly Grey

Fig. 2. Letter asking for information.

5

Interviewing Useful Contacts

APPROACHING YOUR SUBJECT

Interviewing people who have specialist knowledge is a very useful way to obtain information. Most people are willing to talk about their work, their hobbies or their life; very often you can learn something from an interview that you would not glean from books. However, interviewing is a skill that requires preparation and practice. Some people may not wish to give you an interview and in this case, you must respect their wishes.

Making an appointment

Most people lead very busy lives today and it is therefore essential that you contact your subject to make an appointment. It is a good idea to give an idea of the amount of time you might require. Explain that you are a writer and are looking for information on a certain subject or person. Say what you are planning to write and whether you already have a commission. Be specific about the information you require. Should you phone or write to make an appointment?

Phoning your subject

If you phone your subject, you may pick an inconvenient time and therefore lose the chance of an interview. Always be polite and, after saying who you are, ask if it is convenient to talk. If not, inquire when it would be possible.

When you can, explain briefly what you require and ask if you could have an interview. Make sure you have your diary to hand so you can compare dates. Except in rare cases, you should go to the subject's home or office but check if it would be more convenient if you met elsewhere and make appropriate arrangements if you can.

Writing a letter

Writing a letter to ask for an interview has many advantages. It gives the subject time to think and the required information is written down. It is easy to forget what is said on the phone and you can go into more detail in a letter. It is a good idea to suggest three or four possible dates. If these are not suitable, ask politely for alternatives. In the letter include the following:

- your credentials
- what you are planning to write
- what specific information you require
- how you think your subject can help you.

Don't forget to include a stamped addressed envelope for the reply.

PREPARING FOR THE INTERVIEW

It is very important to prepare conscientiously for the interview. Make a list of relevant questions you want to ask. Decide exactly what it is you need to know. What are the gaps in your knowledge that you hope the interviewee will be able to fill?

Asking the right questions

Prepare a number of questions that you hope will lead to the answers you require. Write down as many as possible. You may not need them all but you must be prepared. Write headings for each list of questions and during the interview be prepared to deviate from them where necessary.

If you are planning to interview a number of people on the same subject, prepare the same questions for each so that you can compare the answers. (Questionnaires will be dealt with in the next chapter.)

Sorting out the equipment

Make a list of what you need to take with you and check it off so you don't forget anything vital. You will need:

- a reporter's notebook (it is easy to turn the pages)
- several pens (pens often run out of ink at awkward times)
- a small tape recorder
- several tapes (these, too, may run out)
- a camera (optional).

Not all interviewees will be happy with a tape recorder. You must ask if you may use it and be gracious if permission is refused. Even if a tape recorder is used, do take notes as well in case the tape is damaged.

If you want to take a photograph of your subject, you must ask permission but don't be upset if you are not permitted to. A photograph will not always be relevant to the type of work you are doing.

Dressing appropriately

What you wear may depend to a certain extent on the location of your interview. Go through your wardrobe to find an appropriate outfit. You should be smart and businesslike. Don't wear jeans, t-shirt and trainers if you want to be taken seriously! You must give the impression of being a professional writer even if you are at the beginning of your career and it is the first interview you have done.

Revising the points

- Always make an appointment.

- Writing a letter is better than phoning.

- Before the interview make a list of what you need.

- Check you have all the equipment before you leave.

FACING YOUR SUBJECT

Now it is time for the interview. Are you ready? Have you checked you have everything you need?

Being professional

Even if it is your first interview, you must give an impression of confidence. Allow yourself plenty of time to find the venue so you don't arrive late and flustered. Always be punctual. To be late suggests an unprofessional approach to your work. Check your hair is tidy and no buttons have popped undone! Ladies, make sure you haven't got lipstick on your teeth! Take some deep breaths to calm yourself before you ring the bell.

Putting your subject at ease

Your subject may be as nervous as you are, so spend a few moments chatting about the weather, the surroundings or anything else of no importance. Only when you feel your interviewee is relaxed, should you ask if you may use a tape recorder. If the request is greeted with horror, explain that it will be unobtrusive and will act as a back-up to your notes. If the answer is still in the negative, accept the ruling gracefully and prepare to take detailed notes. If you can do shorthand, it helps, but this is not essential.

Leading your subject

Once the interview has started, you must make it clear, without being too bossy, that you are in charge. Listen to the occasional irrelevant reminiscences but lead firmly but politely back to the main issue.

You do not need to keep rigidly to your questions. Something your subject says may lead to another pertinent question and open up a new line of thought. Although you require certain specific information, do not close your mind to anything else that might be useful – either now or at a future date.

If you have a question to ask that might be controversial but which, for you, is a key question, leave it until the end when your subject is completely relaxed. Then ask it casually as if it is an afterthought and hope you get a useful answer.

CONCLUDING THE INTERVIEW

If you need a photograph, ask for it when you have finished the main part of the interview. Don't be offended if the request is refused. Accept it graciously. It is courteous to let your interviewee see the work before it is published but this is not essential. Some writers refuse to do so on the grounds that often the subject is sometimes too critical of the way something has been written and has little idea of what editors require.

However, if you are writing a factual piece for which you have relied heavily on the interview, you will need to have it checked so that the finished work does not contain errors. In any event, send your subject a copy of the final printed work.

Don't forget to thank your subject for his or her time and hospitality. Ask if a further interview could be granted if necessary. If a subject has been very nervous, a second one might be advantageous as there should be less apprehension after the first.

Revising the points

- Be punctual.

- Be confident and professional.

- Put your subject at ease.

- Keep the interview on the right track.

- Don't forget to thank your subject for the interview.

FOLLOWING THE INTERVIEW

Even though you thanked your subject after the interview, you should still write a letter to thank him or her and say how much you enjoyed the time. Mention a possible follow up if you think it is necessary.

Sorting out your notes

Now comes the hard part. As soon after the interview as possible, you must listen to your tape and sort out your notes. Type them up neatly in the order in which they will be required. This will not necessarily be the order in which the interview progressed.

Slotting in the information

This is the interesting part. Collect all the information you have to date and see where your new material will slot in. Your work is now beginning to take shape.

Revising the points

- Write a letter of thanks.

- Sort out your notes and type them up.

- Decide where they will go in the finished work.

CASE STUDIES

Esther visits the Lord of the Manor

Esther wishes to interview Mrs Bray, the Lord of the Manor of Shere, so she writes the letter in Figure 3.

Mrs Bray agrees to meet Esther on Tuesday morning. Esther arrives on time and enjoys a coffee and some social chit chat before getting down to the questions she wants to ask. Mrs Bray is an easy subject to interview; she is happy with the use of the tape recorder

22 Brandon Hill
Woking
Surrey GU22 7PZ
Tel: (01483) 123456

8 Feb 200X

Dear Mrs Bray

Having been commissioned by *Surrey County Magazine* to write an article on the history of Shere, I wondered if you would allow me to interview you. I am a professional writer and a member of the Society of Women Writers and Journalists. Over the years I have had many feature articles published in a variety of magazines including *The Lady*, *Heritage* and *Surrey County Magazine*.

In the article I would like to include some information on the role of the Lord of the Manor and I hope you will be willing to talk to me about this and also about any interesting experiences you have had in this position.

I hope to visit Shere next week and wondered if any of the following dates would be convenient for me to visit you: the mornings of Tuesday 15 February or Wednesday 16 February or the afternoon of Thursday 17 February.

If none of these is convenient and you are willing to be interviewed, perhaps you would kindly suggest some alternative dates.

I hope it will be possible for us to meet and I enclose an SAE for your convenience.

Yours sincerely

Esther Bywaters

Fig. 3. Letter requesting interview.

but declines to have her picture taken.

Esther is delighted with the result of the interview and, having sorted out her notes, decides where in her article she will include the new information.

Andrew interviews a history lecturer

Andrew has decided to interview the history lecturer, Mr Mann, from the sixth form college he attended. He phones to make an appointment but unfortunately, he does not prepare carefully enough before he goes. He arrives late, having failed to check the bus times, and so gets off to a bad start.

Because Mr Mann taught him, Andrew is nervous and it is the lecturer who tries to put him at his ease. He has only prepared a few questions and as Mr Mann is very garrulous, it is easy for him to dominate the interview instead of Andrew. Much of what he says is not connected to the Second World War during which Andrew's book takes place.

With Mr Mann's permission, Andrew has used a tape recorder but he forgets to insert a new tape and does not bring a spare one. He takes notes but when he gets home, he finds they are almost impossible to read. He feels very discouraged.

Molly chats to some suffragettes

Molly has discovered several elderly ladies who were suffragettes. Five of them are willing to be interviewed. She decides to ask them similar questions. The answers she gets differ greatly. In some cases, this is worrying and Molly has to decide how to use this information. In other cases, the differences are enlightening and she also has some more interesting anecdotes to add to her book.

6

Preparing Questionnaires

INTRODUCING QUESTIONNAIRES

Questionnaires are lists of relevant questions used by researchers to acquire information. They can be used for many purposes. A firm might want to know how clients react to a change in their business proceedings; a charity might need to know how much you know about its work; a student might be doing a thesis on leisure activities; a writer might be researching for a novel and decides to use a questionnaire to find out the interests and habits of a certain group of people in a particular place.

I'm sure you've been asked to fill in one at some time. Researchers waylay you in the street and ask if you can answer some questions. Charities and firms send you questionnaires in the post and ask if you would kindly fill them in to aid their research. Some of the forms are very detailed but they usually only require you to tick an answer so most of your time is spent reading the pamphlet.

Questionnaires are used for a variety of reasons but the one thing they have in common is that they are designed to find out something from a group of people so that the information can be utilised by the questioner.

USING QUESTIONNAIRES EFFECTIVELY

If you wish to obtain information from a large number of people and you cannot interview them all, then questionnaires are the answer.

Targeting the right people
Before you start, decide exactly what it is you need to know and who it is who will have this information. Don't waste time and money by sending questionnaires to people who will be of no help to you. If you already know the people to whom you are going to send questionnaires and there are not many of them, make a list of their addresses and check that you have noted down everyone you need.

It is more likely that you will need to send to a wider group of people. How do you compile your list? Where do you find the people you need?

Compiling your mailing list

There are firms who specialise in compiling mailing lists of people with special interests. Have you ever wondered why you receive so much junk mail? It is probably because you once bought or expressed an interest in a specific product or service. Your name was then added to a list of like-minded people and you are then sent information about related products or services.

The following firm is worth noting as it holds a wide variety of mailing lists. Write or phone to explain what you need and ask what is on offer: Hamilton House Mailings Limited, 17 Staveley Way, Brixworth Industrial Park, Northampton NN6 9TX. Tel: (01604) 881889.

In the *Yellow Pages* you will find a list of local clubs. You may find one that specialises in your subject. Members' lists are today protected by the Data Protection Act but if you phone the Secretary and explain why you would like a list, he or she may be able to help you. Some clubs keep two lists – a complete one and another one omitting the names of members who do not wish their names to be given out.

Distributing your questionnaires

If your questionnaire is to be sent out over a wide area, you will obviously need to use the post. Don't forget to enclose a stamped addressed envelope for the completed forms. You should also include a covering letter explaining who you are and why you would like the questions answered (see Figure 4).

There are, however, cheaper ways of distributing your questionnaires.

Visiting a club

Having decided you wish to write an article on how the over-sixties spend their leisure time, phone the club secretaries of several local Senior Citizens' Clubs. Explain who you are and ask if they would be willing to distribute some questionnaires to their groups. Ask if these could be filled out during the meetings and if so, when it would be convenient for you to collect the papers.

2 Jubilee Gardens
Reading
Berks
RG1 2SE

15 January 200X

The Manager
Sovereign Travel Agency
Stockport
Lancs
ST2 5EA

Dear Sir

I am a freelance writer and have been commissioned by the magazine *Travel News* to write an article on the most popular holiday resorts. So that my article is accurate, I should be most grateful if you could find time to fill in the enclosed questionnaire. It should not take you long and it would be a great help to me. If you felt able to add any additional information, I would appreciate it and in that case, I would acknowledge your contribution in the article.

I enclose an SAE for the return of the questionnaire.

Yours faithfully

Michael Smith

Fig. 4. Example of a covering letter to accompany questionnaire.

Using the library
If you need to discover the reading habits of a group of people, where better to go than your local library? Ask the librarian if you may give out questionnaires to visitors on a certain day. It might be useful to have a table and pencils near the door so the forms can be filled in and dropped into the box you will have prepared. Don't forget to get the librarian's agreement and if you are given a refusal, accept it and rethink your strategy.

Walking round the town

If your project is general and you wish to target a cross-section of the community, why not make a house-to-house delivery? Enclose a covering letter explaining who you are and why you need the information, and explain that you will be back to collect it. Give the date and approximate time you will return. Ask if it could be left outside if that is more convenient.

Getting the timing right

Some questionnaires can be relevant at any time of year. However, if your research deals with a particular time of year, make sure you send out your questionnaires at the appropriate time. If you wish to make a study of how GCSE students study, send out your questionnaire in April or May just before the examinations start.

If you are targeting mothers of school-age children to discover their views about the length of school holidays, use your questionnaires in September when the children will have returned to school and the mothers can relax. Views on Christmas celebrations should be sought during December when the shops are ablaze with decorations and the buying of presents is the main preoccupation of many.

Make your questionnaires fit in with your own timetable. Use them at the time when you are approaching that section of your work. The information will then be fresh in your mind when you have collated it.

However, you should remember that magazines plan their work several months in advance. You may have to send out your questionnaires earlier or write the article the following year.

Revising the points

- Target carefully the people to whom you will send questionnaires.

- Compile a mailing list.

- Save postage by visiting clubs or doing a house-to-house delivery.

- Always include a covering letter.

- Get the timing right.

WRITING THE QUESTIONS

Questionnaires are anonymous so you must not ask the name of the person. However, you are at liberty to ask the age and sex of the person given the questionnaire. This will usually be necessary for your research.

Your questions must be very concise and clear. Before deciding on them, make a list of the information you wish to gather. Then tailor your questions to fit it. Don't have too many. The longer your questionnaire is, the less likely people are to fill it in.

Your questionnaire will be competing with others. You must sell yourself and convince the recipient that yours is the one to fill in. Writers are often regarded as rather 'glamorous' or 'exotic' so remember to explain that you are a writer in your covering letter.

COLLATING THE DATA

Once you have collected all the questionnaires, start to record the data as soon as possible. If you leave it, you may lose the thread of what you had planned to do. Try to do it all without having too many breaks in between. Collating data is not easy and can be very confusing. You should have made it as easy for yourself as possible by the form of your questions.

Once you have collected all the relevant information, organise it and type it out so that it is easy for you to incorporate into your writing.

MAKING USE OF THE INFORMATION

Once you have organised it sensibly, you are ready to use it in your work. As you have spent some time collating it, much of the information will still be in your head and this should make it easier to use.

It is very important to utilise the new material as quickly as possible so that you don't forget what you have done. Even if you don't send out the article for a year, you can still write it.

Revising the points
- Identify the information you need.

- Make your questions clear and concise.

- Collate the data and use it as soon as possible.

CASE STUDIES

Molly targets some suffragettes

Molly has had a very helpful letter from the lady in Scotland who has provided her with some valuable information. She has also interviewed other suffragettes but decides it would be a good idea to give some questionnaires to others she has discovered. Some of them live some distance away from her so she posts the questionnaires remembering to include a covering letter and a stamped addressed envelope.

Some letters she delivers personally and in some cases she finds it helpful to go over the questions. One lady is blind so Molly reads her the questions and notes down her answers.

She also visits several senior citizens' clubs and gives questionnaires to any ladies over 90 (see Figure 5). She is amazed how many there are and how active their brains still are.

---

1. What is your age?

2. Were you a suffragette?

3. If not, were you sympathetic to the movement?

4. Was anyone in your family a suffragette?

5. Did you ever meet any suffragettes?

6. If you were a suffragette, were you ever imprisoned?

7. How long for?

8. How many times?

9. Were you force fed?

10. Do you still suffer as a result of your imprisonment?

11. Was it worth it?

12. Were the men in your family sympathetic to the movement?

13. If yes, did they actively help in it?

14. If no, were they (a) strongly against it? (b) passive?

Fig. 5. Molly's senior citizens' questionnaire.

1. Are you male or female?

2. What is your age?

3. What subjects are you studying?

4. Have you heard of the suffragettes?

5. Who was their leader?

6. Write down four points about them.

7. Are you grateful for what they did?

8. Did you vote in the last election?

9. If yes, why?

10. If no, why not?

Fig. 6. Molly's college questionnaire.

Molly also decides to target further education colleges to see what the students know about the suffragettes (see Figure 6).

Andrew visits a senior citizens' club

After his unsuccessful interview, Andrew decides to visit a senior citizens' club and ask if he can give out a simple questionnaire. He rings up the secretary of the local 'Silver Circle Club' and is told that the club is to hold a 'Remembrance Meeting' the following week. What he proposes will fit in with it and the Secretary agrees to his visit. He is delighted.

The club has about thirty members so Andrew produces thirty-five questionnaires and remembers to take the same number of pencils. He finds a bargain shop where he can buy them cheaply.

He wishes to acquire some personal stories of the Second World War that he can adapt for his novel. His questionnaire is a little different as he wishes each person who fills in a questionnaire to write an anecdote about the war that is still vivid to him or her (see Figure 7). He hopes this will work.

Not all the members are happy to fill in the forms although some of them are happy to tell him their stories. He is relieved he has

1. Are you male or female?

2. How old are you?

3. How old were you when the Second World War started?

4. Were you frightened during the Battle of Britain?

5. What were you doing during this time?

6. Where did you go when there was an air raid?

7. Please write down briefly anything that happened to you or near you during the war that you still remember vividly.

Fig. 7. Andrew's questionnaire about the Second World War.

taken pen and paper to the meeting. About twenty members are present and more than half of them spend some time writing their stories.

When Andrew looks at the forms, he is delighted to discover he has a variety of stories. Some who filled them in had been children, others had been in the Services and some were housewives who had had their lives disrupted by having evacuees foisted on them. One of them had been a Battle of Britain pilot. He is sure he can incorporate the stories into his novel.

7

Soaking Yourself in the Atmosphere

OBSERVING YOUR SETTING

Whether you are writing a novel, biography or article, nothing can take the place of visiting the places you are writing about. It can be time consuming but you will discover a wealth of detail which would not have been available otherwise.

Exploring the area

Visiting a village
If you are writing about a small village, walk around it. Explore the tiny lanes and study the type of houses. Notice how many shops there are and what they sell. Is there much traffic passing through? Do tourists visit it?

Is it on a bus route? How easy is it to get to the nearest town by public transport? Is there a train station? How old is the village?

Visiting a town
Because a town is bigger, there will be more to see and more distance to cover. If your novel requires your character to travel, study the bus routes and the bus and train timetables. Make sure you check what train journeys can be made from your town. If you make a mistake, someone is sure to point it out. Travel on the buses and trains to discover how crowded they are at certain times of the day. Find out how long journeys take. It is the attention to detail that will give your work the professional touch.

Talking to people

Don't forget to talk to people. They will provide first-hand information about the area. You may be told by the village postmistress that there are now only two collections of mail a day while there used to be three.

Someone waiting at the bus stop may complain that bus times have been reorganised and she finds it difficult to get to the nearest town.

Using the experts
As well as the area itself, you may need to find out more about the work your character does. Talk to doctors, nurses, teachers, caretakers, shop assistants, secretaries and factory workers to find out about their jobs. Visit a factory to get the 'feel' of it. If you wish to do this, don't forget to phone to make an appointment. Most places will be happy for you to visit and this will make your work come alive because you will have more idea what your characters are experiencing.

Attending events
If there are festivals, fairs or celebrations that take place in the area you are writing about, then do try to visit them. You may be able to incorporate them into your novel or biography. Having first-hand experience of an event will mean that you can write about it more vividly. Don't forget to take notes. It is very easy to forget your first impressions.

Using the senses
In any piece of writing, using the senses brings your work alive. Make notes on the visual impact of a river glistening in the sunlight. How do the hills change colour as dark clouds sweep across the sky? Think of some unusual comparisons.

What about smells? Does your character go into a baker's shop to buy bread in the early morning when the bread has been freshly baked? Experience it yourself and create a striking image to enable your reader to *smell* the new bread.

Don't forget taste and touch. Neither is necessarily pleasant and to evoke an unpleasant taste is just as important.

Homing in on the sounds
Shut your eyes and listen. You will be amazed at the variety of sounds you will hear. Try to identify them and write down a phrase to remind you.

If you have a small tape recorder with you, put it on and record the sounds you hear. If you are attending a festival or procession of some kind, there will probably be a band so it would definitely be an advantage to record that. Morris dancing is done to particular sounds. You may be able to record the bells around the dancers' feet, actuated by their stamping. Would you remember how it sounded it you hadn't recorded it?

Sometimes you can buy records, cassettes or compact discs of local dances, choirs and festivals.

Making notes

Taking notes on the spot is important as it is always difficult to remember exactly a sight, smell or sound. While you are soaking in the atmosphere of a place, fill your notebook with images. They will be an invaluable aid to your writing.

Type them up when you get home while they are still fresh in your memory. You may be able to add an appropriate word or phrase. Then when you come to write, you have a store of vivid impressions on which to draw.

Revising the points

- Note down details.

- Check the bus routes and timetables.

- Talk to people.

- Use the experts.

- Attend events.

- Use your senses.

TAKING PHOTOGRAPHS

Even if you are not a very good photographer, taking photographs is a bonus. Take as many as you can of the area at different times of the day. In colour photographs you will see how the light changes. If you are able to visit several times, you will probably have the opportunity to see your locations when it is sunny or dull, raining or threatening to rain. It is also a good idea to take photographs at different times of the year. In the summer a park appears very different from how it is in the winter. In spring the colours are bright and fresh; in autumn, they are muted.

Not every piece of writing will lend itself to the study of photographs. But you may find that your store of photos can be used later in a different piece.

Using your photographs

Some of the photographs you take may be used in the book or article you are writing. Check what type of photo is required before spending money on film. Do they require transparencies or are colour prints acceptable? It is worth providing your own photos as magazines often pay more for the photograph than they do for the text! Publishers often ask for photographs on CD Rom nowadays. A good photographic shop can put your negatives on this.

Your photos will also provide you with an excellent research aid. You may be writing your article some time after your visit. Your photos will provide you with an immediate recollection of your visit and you can see exactly where the post office is in relation to the coffee shop. It is unlikely you would remember such a detail without your pictures.

STUDYING THE AREA

You will have done a certain amount of 'studying' when actually in the area. But when you are sitting at your desk, you will have further opportunity to study the material you have accumulated. If you have not been able to visit the location, the material you have been able to buy will be vital. Write to the nearest tourist agency to ask for any information. Some you will receive free but guidebooks and postcards you will have to buy. Don't forget to enclose a stamped addressed envelope when writing for information.

Reading guidebooks

Buy all the guidebooks you can. They will be extremely useful. As well as telling you the history of the area, they will give you a detailed description. However, do check the information is up to date.

Guides to churches, museums and stately homes will also be useful. They will provide more detail than you could absorb in a single visit.

Using maps

Maps are also an essential part of your research equipment. Again, make sure they are up to date. New roads are being built all the time and it is easy to make a mistake. Make sure you know which roads lead out of your town or village and where they go. Check a map of the area for the time about which you are writing. If you have your characters driving on motorways in the 1920s, your work will lack authenticity!

Looking at postcards and pictures

Most places now have a collection of local postcards. If the area is a popular tourist attraction, there will be a great variety from the comic to the picturesque. Study the cards for specific detail. If you have been unable to visit the area, the pictures will be of even more value.

Sometimes local artists have painted their favourite views. These may be expensive to buy but occasionally postcard reproductions will be available. You may also be able to visit an exhibition of local paintings. Some of these at least will be of nearby scenes.

Buying local newspapers and magazines

Buying local newspapers and magazines is a bonus. You will learn a lot about the area and the people who live in it. You may even find some incidents you could use in your work. Perhaps you will learn about someone who would be worth visiting. The possibilities are endless.

Revising the points

- Take plenty of photographs.

- Buy guidebooks, maps and postcards.

- Be accurate.

- Buy local newspapers and magazines.

CASE STUDIES

Esther walks round Shere

Esther pays another visit to Shere. She has found a book describing the houses in Shere and discovers that almost every one has a history. Although she may not use all the material, she walks around the village stopping at most of the houses and reading about them. Many of them are very old.

Talking to a local resident, she hears that there are many people in the village whose families have lived there for generations. Others are newcomers and Esther discovers that when the houses are bought, the new owners may alter the inside but they are not allowed to change the outside at all. In this way the character of the village is preserved.

She takes as many photos as she can. Knowing that the editor of *Surrey County Magazine* prefers transparencies, she takes two cameras. In one she puts a film for slides. With this she takes photos to illustrate her article. In the other she has a colour print film. These photographs she will use for her own study purposes.

Tucked away at the top of a hill beside another cottage is the small museum. This is a treasure trove of artefacts ancient and not so ancient. A real find is a sixteenth-century gentleman's hat which, the curator tells Esther, was discovered behind the wall of one of the cottages when some repair work was being done. It has recently been restored by the British Museum. Esther receives permission to photograph it and is sure it will find a place in her article.

She is very pleased with her day's work and decides to treat herself to a cream tea at the village café which at one time was the post office and is one of the oldest buildings in the village. Esther is disappointed to discover a few months later that it is no longer a café. While eating her cream tea, she studies her notes and organises them ready for typing.

Andrew visits Coventry
Andrew has decided to set his Second World War novel in Coventry. He hopes he will get plenty of first-hand information as it was badly bombed during the war. He visits it and buys a book entitled *Coventry during the War*. There are a number of guidebooks and in a secondhand shop he is delighted to find some old postcards of Coventry before the war. There are also some black and white photographs taken just after the terrible blitz. These are rather expensive but Andrew feels they will be extremely useful.

He chats to the elderly man behind the counter and learns that he was in Coventry during the war. Explaining that he is writing a book, Andrew asks if the man can remember a lot about it. He is delighted that his question leads to a fund of reminiscences which Andrew is sure he will be able to use. He wishes he'd brought a tape recorder. He is also told which places to look for and sets off to walk round the city. He tries to imagine himself wandering around in 1940. Because of the bustling, modern city, he finds it hard. He skirts the cathedral and decides he will visit that on another occasion.

Molly follows the suffragette route
Molly is spending another day in London. She has decided to visit some of the places where the suffragettes held meetings. She also stands outside the Houses of Parliament trying to imagine what it felt like to chain yourself to the railings for your beliefs. Would she have done the same thing? She wanders towards Downing Street and then decides to follow the so-called 'Mud March' of three thousand

women in 1907 through the streets of London. She doesn't complete it and arrives home exhausted but with some idea how the suffragettes felt.

The following week she spends a night in Manchester. She visits the Free Trade Hall where Christabel Pankhurst and Annie Kenney attempted to address a meeting. Molly tries to imagine how they felt when they were unceremoniously flung out and then arrested. She becomes increasingly grateful for what they suffered so that she could have the vote and decides that the last chapter of her book has to be about the result of the suffragette movement.

8

Reliving the Past

VISITING HISTORIC BUILDINGS

Much can be learned from visiting old buildings. There is a wealth of them throughout this land and in them you can find portraits, furniture and books as well as valuable old documents and other items of interest.

Visiting stately homes

If you are a member of the National Trust, you will have free access to a number of stately homes. These can provide you with a great deal of information. The rooms will be set out as they were in a bygone age and if there are not too many visitors, it is easy to people the area with costumed characters of long ago.

Some stately homes are still owned by the families in whose possession they have been for many centuries. In this case you could write to the owners and ask for more information about their past lifestyle. Explain that you are a writer and you wish to make your novel or article as authentic as possible. You may be able to see areas not open to the general public and to hear at first hand about an earlier lifestyle.

Taking photographs

You may not be permitted to take photographs inside the house. Flash, like sunlight, fades the delicate fabrics and paintings. This is the reason why most rooms in stately homes are quite dark. However, you can certainly photograph the house from the outside and the grounds and you *may* be granted permission to take a photograph inside.

If you wish to include in your work a photograph of the inside of the house, ask the owner if they will permit you to take photographs or, if not, ask if they have one you can use. In the case of National Trust properties, there is a policy that must be adhered to by all photographers. The National Trust has asked that it be included in this book so it is set out below.

National Trust policy on commercial photography
Commercial photographers are at liberty to photograph National Trust landscape and coastline, except where they are undertaking a commission for product or service advertising. However, they are advised to contact the Regional Public Affairs Manager (RPAM) should they wish to take pictures on land that contains Sites of Scientific Interest. The same applies if they wish to take pictures of listed species. A list of the names and addresses of the RPAMs is available from the Trust's Central Photographic Library.

For commercial photography of gardens, architectural exteriors and interiors, permission is required from the RPAM. If permission is given, the photographers are asked to confirm in writing that the pictures are for one-time use only and invited to consider lodging appropriate images in the Central Photographic Library on the usual 50/50 basis. Photography for other photo libraries is never permitted.

The library holds mixed-format transparencies by leading specialist photographers comprising landscape, coastline, agriculture, architecture, interiors, gardens, paintings conservation and environment. All income from the Photo Library is re-invested in continuing the work of the Trust.

National Trust policy on amateur photography
Amateur photography is welcomed out-of-doors at the properties. Should you wish to use a tripod or monopod you must check first with the property. Photography is not permitted indoors when houses are open to visitors. However, special arrangements can be made for interested amateurs to take interior photographs by appointment outside normal opening hours. Applications must be made in writing to the property concerned, for a mutually convenient appointment. There is an admission charge for this facility and this also applies to National Trust members.

British Association of Picture Libraries and Agencies
To find out about photo libraries and how they work contact the British Association of Picture Libraries and Agencies at 18 Vine Hill, London EC1R 5DX. Tel: (020) 7713 1780.

Buying guidebooks
There will usually be a glossy guidebook of the house which will contain a number of photographs and detailed information about the history of the house and the people who lived in it. There will also sometimes be postcards and slides.

Visiting churches and cathedrals

As well as the parish records, which have already been mentioned in Chapter 2, much can be learned from the tombs and memorials of the church and the graves in the churchyard. Many are very old and if you are tracing a family history, this may be the place to start. It may also give you an idea for a novel or a short story.

There should be no problem taking photographs both inside and outside the church or cathedral. Often there are guidebooks and postcards to help your research. Wander round the churchyard and look at the tombstones. First names quickly go out of fashion and the names on graves can often help you to choose appropriate names for your characters.

You may also find some amusing epitaphs or unusual stones. If you notice something interesting, make a note. You may be able to use it at a later date even if it is not applicable for your present work.

Visiting inns and hotels

Many of our inns date back centuries and few of them discard their ancient history. You will find fascinating stories in every corner and the proprietor may be able to tell you interesting anecdotes not found in any guidebook. If you can use them, this will add authenticity to your work.

You may be able to get a free night's lodging if you explain you are writing a book or an article and a particular inn or hotel will be featured in it. Many writers use this facility, but make sure you visit out of season and not in the busy tourist season. Never expect to stay more than two nights in one hotel. You may be offered bed and breakfast accommodation but you should pay for any other meals you have.

Finding monuments and plaques

The British are very good at identifying places where something of importance has happened. Plaques on walls of houses will indicate where someone was born, lived or died. Monuments identify battlegrounds. The areas will have changed beyond all recognition but as you stand on the site of a hard fought battle, try to conjure up the sights and sounds of that terrible time.

Revising the points

- Ask if you may take photographs.

- Check National Trust policy on taking photographs.

- Buy guidebooks.
- Be aware of the unusual.

STUDYING COSTUME

If you are writing about a period other than your own, it is very important that the costume is correct. There are so many details that need to be researched if your work is to be authentic. There are many books which will give you a history of costume and these are very valuable. But as well as studying books, there are other ways of checking on costume.

Looking at portraits

Before photography, those who could afford it had their portraits painted. Portrait painting was a very lucrative business in the sixteenth, seventeenth and eighteenth centuries. With the introduction of photography, its popularity waned but even today portrait painters are commissioned to paint famous people to celebrate particular occasions.

The National Portrait Gallery in St Martin's Place, London – just around the corner from the National Gallery in Trafalgar Square – has portraits dating back to the twelfth century. As portraits are always contemporary, the detail of the costume is always painstakingly done. Take your notebook and make notes of the type of dress your subject may have worn to go to a ball. You will also be able to discover how her hair was done and what shoes she was wearing.

If you are writing a biography, you might be lucky enough to find a portrait of your subject. However, it should be remembered that portraits were usually painted to flatter the subject so although there was some similarity of feature, the face was not always accurate. Henry VIII, having seen a portrait of his prospective bride, Anne of Cleves, was impressed by her beauty. But when he saw the real Anne, he was horrified to discover she looked like 'a Flanders mare', as he rudely remarked.

You can usually buy postcards of a variety of the portraits on show. No gallery has all its pictures on show so if there is something that you wish to see that is not on view, do ask. It is wise to phone first in case it has to be unearthed.

Discovering costume museums

Unlike armour and 'hard' artefacts, costume, unfortunately, wears out so it is very difficult to find any original costumes further back than the eighteenth century. Sometimes it is easier to find children's clothes because they grow out of their garments and so only wear them for a very short time.

One of the best costume museums is in Bath. This is the Museum of Costume and Fashion Research Centre. If you need help with your research, write first to The Keeper of Fashion, 4 Circus Road, Bath, North Somerset BA1 2EW. Tel: (01225) 477752. The museum offers study facilities.

The Victoria and Albert Museum in London also houses a collection of costume and Kensington Palace has a display of court dresses from 1750. Many stately homes also have small costume collections and you will often find a few genuine garments in small local museums. Not all their possessions will be on show so do ask if they have other dresses you can see. They will be very happy to help you; the assistants are always delighted to talk to anyone who takes a sincere interest in aspects of their work.

Another useful visit you could make would be to Madame Tussaud's Waxwork Museum. Here you can see costumes on models of the real people; this is much more realistic than seeing a picture or a costume on a hanger. The more modern the character is, the greater the likeness, but even Henry VIII and his six wives look very like the portraits we have seen of them.

If you are writing a biography of someone who is displayed in the museum, you can study the features and expression – something it is more difficult to do if you are talking to the real person.

Talking with the wardrobe mistress

Theatre companies will usually have access to a vast wardrobe. The National Theatre and the BBC, in particular, produce costumes for the period plays they do. Sometimes these go on show and the displays are always worth a visit.

The wardrobe mistress or her assistants will know a great deal about period costume as they have to be accurate. They are very busy people but there is nothing to stop you phoning to ask if you could talk to one of them. You might even be able to watch the costumes being made. They will probably use modern fastenings but there are some open air museums where the costumes and the lifestyle are as authentic as it is possible to make them. There will be more about these in the next section.

Many counties have a theatre wardrobe which hires out costumes to amateur dramatic societies. Why not hire a costume for a day or two and wear it around the house to see how it feels?

Browsing in secondhand shops
Secondhand shops are always worth a visit. You won't want to spend a fortune on costume but you may find some genuine articles that are very inexpensive. It might be helpful to hold something to give you the feel of the period. How does it feel to hold a fan? Can you flick it open as to the manner born? How did they manage their swords? Was it as easy as it looks to pull a sword out of its scabbard? What about sitting down with a sword dangling at your left side?

Filing your material
It is very useful to keep a scrapbook of costume so you can study the pictures at your leisure. Cut out anything relevant you find in magazines and newspapers and paste them into a book with any postcards you have acquired. Keep a separate folder of useful booklets you have bought at museums and stately homes.

Revising the points
- Check all costume details.
- Buy postcards and guidebooks.
- File your material.

RESEARCHING SOCIAL CUSTOMS

If you are writing about a period other than your own, whether you are writing fiction or non-fiction, you will need to create the flavour of the period. You must know how your characters travelled, what they ate, what leisure activities they enjoyed and what they talked about. If you are researching the nineteenth and early twentieth centuries and you need to know about the life of servants during that period, the National Trust has produced an excellent book, *Not in Front of the Servants* by Frank Victor Dawes. The author advertised for reminiscences from anyone who had been in domestic service and he was inundated with replies. The resulting book provides a fascinating insight into 'downstairs' life until the Second World War radically changed society.

Playing a role
If your period is the sixteenth century and you really want to know

what it feels like to live in that century, you could not do better than visit Kentwell Hall at Long Milford in Suffolk. They do historical re-creations of the sixteenth century. For three weeks in June and July you can live as close as possible to the way the people lived in a particular year of that century. Each member who takes part in the 'great annual re-creation' has a particular role to play and job to do. The costumes, food, living conditions and even speech are as authentic as possible. There is a training day beforehand when you will be told which role you are to play and what costume you are to wear. This you have to make yourself. There are no short cuts. You can't use Velcro and zip fasteners! They didn't have those in the sixteenth century. You must sew on buttons and make button holes or stitch on tapes for tying.

If you can't manage to give up three weeks in the interests of research, you could go for a shorter period, or you could just visit the site at weekends and watch the inhabitants at work and leisure. You may even talk to them but don't mention telephones and televisions. They won't know what you are talking about!

As well as the two weeks in June, there are other re-creations during selected weekends in May, August and September. Write or phone for information. The address is: Kentwell Hall Historical Re-creations, Long Milford, Suffolk CO10 9BA. Tel: (01787) 310207.

Eating meals

There are a number of books which will tell you about the food of the day but one of the best resources is a collection of booklets produced by English Heritage entitled *Food and Cooking in Britain*. There are seven booklets. The first three give information about prehistoric Britain, Roman Britain and the medieval period. The other four deal with the sixteenth to the nineteenth centuries. Each booklet describes the meals, the tableware, the cooking methods and the utensils used. There are helpful illustrations and a number of recipes of the time.

Another useful book is *The National Trust Book of Christmas and Festive Day Recipes*. As well as the recipes, the book contains some useful information on customs.

You can also visit kitchens in stately homes and inspect their cooking facilities. Sometimes there will be wax food on display to suggest what might have been cooked.

Changing behaviour

Styles of behaviour and manners change over the centuries. Jane

Austen and Charles Dickens will give you some indication of the customs of their times. *A Punch History of Manners 1841–1940* by A. Adburgham, published by Hutchinson, would also be useful. To study manners further back in time *The Polite World* by J. Wildeblood and P. Brinson, published by the Oxford University Press, covers the thirteenth to the nineteenth centuries.

Travelling round the country

Methods of transport have also varied throughout the centuries. At one time the rivers were used a great deal more than they are now and roads were often little more than mud tracks. People were not free to move around the country as we do today. A journey of a few miles would have been a great undertaking involving considerable planning and it may have taken days to cover the distance. Many people would never leave their villages.

Using horses

If a long journey was made by horseback, it would have been necessary for the horses to rest as a horse can only travel for a certain length of time before dropping dead from exhaustion! Carriage horses were usually changed at posting inns. Carriages were always being modified so it is important to check that the right mode of transport is being used in your book. You should also check how long a particular journey would take. Stage coaches for public use were drawn by eight horses and took weeks to travel what today would take hours.

Alan Sutton Publishers Ltd (Phoenix Mill, Far Thrupp, Stroud, Gloucester GL5 2BU) are specialists in transport books so it would be worthwhile to send for a catalogue to see what they have on offer that could help you.

The advent of the railway

The building of railways made it easier for people to travel around the country and there is no shortage of railway books and museums to give you information on their past glory. In some museums you can get a flavour of the old days by travelling on one of the old steam trains that has been saved for posterity.

The introduction of the motor vehicle

Motors cars, too, made travelling easier for those who could afford to buy these new contraptions. There are a number of motor museums where you can browse and get the feel of the early motor car. You should be able to find plenty of information on petrol consumption, mileage and different types of cars. One of the most famous museums is the Beaulieu Motor Museum.

In the London Transport Museum in Covent Garden you can see the early buses and trams and listen to recordings of what it was like to be a bus driver or a 'clippy' in the early days.

Enjoying leisure

Radio and television is a very recent innovation. In past days people would have had to make their own entertainment at home. Sometimes, however, there would be fairs and festivals which would be the highlight of the village year and all the villagers would join in the celebrations.

It should not be difficult to find books about fairs and festivals in different countries. Your local library will help you and you may find a little gem in your local secondhand bookshop.

Sporting activities

There were always sporting activities that men could enjoy either as participants or as spectators. These were often confined to certain classes. It is important to remember that class played an important part in society until the advent of the two world wars. The series *A History of Everyday Things in England*, published by B. T. Batsford Ltd, is a mine of information about all aspects of life in the various centuries. Asa Briggs has also written a book, *How They Lived: 1700–1815*, published by Blackwell.

Going to church

For centuries the church was the centre of life in the village. It would be expected that everyone would go to church on a Sunday dressed up in their best clothes; they would sit or stand in their allotted places with the squire and his family sitting in the front pews. Don't have your characters going out to enjoy themselves on a Sunday if you are writing a period piece!

GETTING THE FLAVOUR OF THE LANGUAGE

Language constantly changes. New words are frequently introduced while others are lost or change their meaning. If you are setting your novel in a certain century or writing a biography of someone long dead, it is important to suggest a different language style. Different words would have been used and the pronunciation would have been different. It is better not to attempt to reproduce the latter. Until the twentieth century there were no recorders to retain voices for posterity. However, while not trying to emulate novelists of earlier centuries, it is a good idea to trawl ideas from them.

Reading the classics
Reading Charles Dickens and Jane Austen will give you a vivid picture of the times in which they were written and the language of the day. Their novels were contemporary so you can get an idea of the type of life people lived at the time. Dickens has created a wealth of characters from different walks of life and his dialogue is worth studying. There is great opportunity for research in his books.

Jane Austen dealt mainly with the emerging middle class and her preoccupation with love and marriage gives an insight into one of the issues that was so important when women were not able to follow careers. Her language is different from that of Dickens. There is not so much variety but it still repays study.

Other classic novelists are also worth studying for detail. Their comments and the details about the lifestyle of their characters can be very valuable for the novelist or biographer. It is worth noting down words and phrases that were in common use in case you might be able to use them.

Using diaries and letters
Both diaries and letters will help in the study of the language of the time. Samuel Pepys' diary of the late seventeenth century is fascinating reading and provides a wealth of detail about London after the Restoration of Charles II. You can almost hear him talking to you as you read it.

Watching plays
Plays written during the period you are writing about can be helpful. If you can manage to watch some on stage, that is a bonus as you will hear how the language sounded, although the pronunciation may not be authentic. Even if you can't see them, obtain a number of them from your local library and read them aloud. Invite your friends round for a play reading. Research can be fun!

The London Academy of Music and Dramatic Art has produced a booklet called *Speeches from the Classics* and includes speeches from the Greek dramatists to Sheridan in the eighteenth century. Reading these aloud will help you to understand the way people spoke.

However, it must be remembered that the language in a play is always slightly artificial as indeed will be the dialogue you write.

CONTACTING YOUR LOCAL HISTORICAL SOCIETY

Most towns have a local historical society and while you are researching, it might be worth joining it so that you can meet experts who have an interest in a particular field. There are usually lectures and slide shows and you might find one that fits in with your requirements.

CHECKING YOUR FACTS

Whatever you are writing, it is vital that your facts are accurate and that you pay attention to detail.

Avoiding anachronisms

An anachronism is something that is out of place because it would not have been known at the time. You can't have your heroine riding a bicycle in the eighteenth century because there were no bicycles then. Do check that the dress fastening, material, machinery or mode of transport was actually used during your period. If you make a mistake, someone is bound to tell you.

A very useful book to help you to avoid the pitfalls of anachronisms is *The New Shell Book of Firsts* published by Headline.

Revising the points

- Pay attention to detail.

- Get your facts right.

- Contact your local historical society.

- Talk to the experts.

- Get the feel of the language.

- Avoid anachronisms.

CASE STUDIES

Esther visits St James Church, Shere

Esther has decided to visit St James Church in Shere. Wandering round it, she discovers an ancient document attached to the wall near a quatrefoil (a small opening shaped like a four-leaved clover). She discovers that in the fourteenth century Christine, a carpenter's daughter, had had herself walled up in a cell adjoining the church. She did this voluntarily so she would worship God and pray with no distractions. She was called an anchoress.

Excited, Esther takes some photographs and makes some notes; she is pleased to find there is a transcript of the document she can buy. She also invests in a guidebook of the church. Returning home, she studies the document. Christine's story she finds fascinating as the girl managed to escape from her self-imposed isolation. But then she repented of her 'sin' of escaping and was walled up again.

Esther makes notes on Christine's story. She will certainly use it in her article and perhaps write another article entirely about Christine.

Molly searches for photographs

Molly has visited the home of one of the founders of the suffragette movement. The house is now owned by the National Trust and there is a lot of memorabilia about the lady herself and the movement.

Molly asks the curator if she may take photographs to illustrate a book she is writing but is told that permission cannot be given without reference to the National Trust. She buys some of the slides on sale and is told that the photographer is local and has a shop in the High Street.

She visits him and explains her dilemma. He is very helpful and says he is quite happy for her to use his work provided she acknowledges it. However, as he was commissioned by the National Trust to take the photos, he feels she should consult the Trust as they own the copyright.

The next day Molly phones the Trust and is told that the photos may be used and the Trust will negotiate a fee with the publisher of her book.

Andrew stays at an inn and visits a museum

A friend has told Andrew that he might be able to obtain a night's free accommodation in a pub or hotel in Coventry if he chooses his time right and explains he is writing a book and will mention the inn in it.

With trepidation he writes a letter to the proprietor of a pub that was bombed during the war and rebuilt soon afterwards incorporating some of the original buildings (see Figure 8).

Dear Mr James

I am a freelance writer and I am currently writing a novel set during the Second World War. It is mainly based in Coventry and I understand that the 'Coach and Horses' was bombed during the war and rebuilt in the same style incorporating some of the original building.

Would it be possible for me to have free accommodation for one night in return for giving publicity to your inn in my book?

I enclose a stamped addressed envelope in the hope that you might be able to help me.

Yours sincerely

Andrew Brown

Fig. 8. Andrew's letter asking for free accommodation.

Andrew is delighted when Mr James agrees to his request as it is out of season. He spends a very pleasant evening chatting with Mr and Mrs James. He is also able to speak to some of the regulars who remember the awful night Coventry was bombed.

The following week he visits the London Transport Museum in London and listens to recordings of bus drivers and conductors giving their accounts of what it was like in London during the Blitz. He feels he is acquiring a lot of material that will make his novel authentic.

9

Travelling the World

If you are an addictive traveller, you will by now have acquired a variety of brochures, magazines, postcards and other useful material.

FILING YOUR MATERIAL

Do make sure you file your material in the way that is best for you. Do this as soon as you return from a trip. Don't fling all you collect in a cupboard and leave the filing until later! You will waste a great deal of time when you need to find a particular brochure or postcard.

Filing material by country is quite useful. You then have everything on a particular place together. You could put it in a large envelope, a cardboard envelope file or even a shoe box. Remember to write what it is on the outside.

You might like to keep separate files for transport, buildings, churches or other categories. It's entirely up to you how you file your material as long as you *do* file it.

USING TRAVEL AGENTS

While it is better to visit a place about which you are writing, it is not essential. There is a vast amount of material on tap for you and even if you are an enthusiastic traveller, you will still need to do other research.

Travel agents are usually very happy to part with a variety of brochures. Tell them what you are doing and they will search for what you need. Sometimes they hold travel evenings with slide shows and talks from people who have visited a particular place. You can pick up a great deal of information from these.

You will also, of course, collect brochures and other information from the places you visit.

CONTACTING TOURIST OFFICES

London contains tourist information offices from many countries. These are listed in the London telephone directory (available in your local library). If you write or phone, they will send you a pack of material about their country. They may also allow you to use their photographs provided an acknowledgement is given. As they are receiving free publicity from your article or book, there is not usually a charge for these.

Embassies and high commissions also have press offices and these can also be helpful. The London Diplomatic List published by The Stationery Office should also be available in your library. This will give the addresses of the embassies and high commissions. It will also provide names. Make a note of the person you need to write to. The personal approach is always the best and by contacting the person by name, there is more chance of your enquiry being dealt with promptly.

EXPLORING TRANSPORT

If your setting is a foreign country, it is likely that your characters will have had to travel from Britain to their destination. Whether your work is modern or period, you must be accurate about your mode of transport.

Travelling by ship

Sea travel has changed radically during this century. If you have travelled on a ship recently and your characters are taking a similar trip, your own notes about your journey will be a great help.

However, if you are writing about an earlier period, you will need to do some research. Look in your local library for appropriate material and if you can't find anything, ask the librarian.

There is a maritime museum in Swansea and the Admiral Blake Museum in Bridgwater, Somerset may be worth a visit. If your characters are going on a cruise a very useful book is *World Cruising Handbook* by Jimmy Cornell, published by A. & C. Black.

Travelling by air

It is not difficult to research a trip by air for your characters. You have probably flown yourself. Take note of the uniform of the stewardesses, what the captain says, what the food is like and any other relevant details. Airlines vary so if you intend to write about a particular airline, write to the publicity office of the airline and ask for information. They will be most helpful if you explain that they will receive free publicity by a mention in your book or article. You will need to know times of flights and how long journeys take. Don't forget about the time change on a long flight.

Seasons vary too. If your characters fly to Australia for Christmas, they may be eating their Christmas lunch on the beach underneath a blazing sun, instead of in front of a log fire.

If you prefer to create an airline of your own, you will still need to know how airlines function and you will presumably use real airports. You always have a long wait for a flight so watch the people and make notes that you may be able to use.

Discovering a variety of planes

Perhaps you need to research the early history of aviation. Search your library or secondhand bookshops for useful books or pamphlets.

If you want to see some of the early planes at close quarters, visit the Fleet Air Arm Museum at Yeovilton in Somerset. Here you can see a variety of planes including some used during both world wars.

There is also a model of Concorde so if you've always fancied a trip on this luxurious plane, now's your chance. You can stroll through the entire plane, including the cockpit, at your leisure.

STUDYING MAPS AND GUIDEBOOKS

If your character is travelling, you will need to check a map for distances and roads. If you are writing a contemporary piece, you must use an up-to-date map.

Up-to-date guidebooks are also helpful. The small *Berlitz Travel Guides* to various countries provide a wealth of information and are handy to carry around.

COLLECTING SOUVENIRS

It is rare to go on holiday without bringing back souvenirs which remind you of the place you have visited. You could even base a short story or an article on an unusual souvenir. Try to collect items that are native to the country so if you are writing a travel article, you can help to evoke the atmosphere of the place by looking at and touching your souvenir.

DELVING INTO DIARIES

Reading the diaries and letters of travellers can provide some interesting ideas. In 1989 the BBC produced a fascinating book entitled *With Passport and Parasol*. Excerpts from the diaries of several Victorian lady travellers provide invaluable reading for the researcher.

REVISING THE POINTS

- File your material appropriately.
- Write to a *named person* at a tourist office.
- Research methods of travelling.
- Buy native souvenirs.

CASE STUDY

Andrew visits the Fleet Air Arm Museum

Andrew's book is progressing well. His main character, Ralph, is a Battle of Britain pilot so Andrew visits the Fleet Air Arm Museum. He makes detailed notes about the type of plane Ralph would have flown and is able to sit in the cockpit to get the feel of the aircraft.

10

Doing Things Your Way

Although there are certain guidelines to follow when doing your research, you don't have to adhere rigidly to them.

FINDING YOUR LEVEL

Research should be fun – not a chore. If you are very shy and feel that you don't relate very well to people, you might prefer to be an 'armchair researcher'. Instead of going out and interviewing someone, you might prefer to use letters and diaries if writing a biography. If your work is factual, you could find your material from a book rather than a person. However, talking to people for your research might bring you out of your shell.

If you interview your subject, should you use a tape or rely on your notes? Again, you must do whatever is most comfortable for you. If you are not happy with tape recorders, databases and the Internet, don't use them. It's not obligatory. You should enjoy whatever you do. You might find you have hidden talents.

RESEARCHING FOR YOUR NOVEL

Much of what has been said in earlier chapters is relevant to the novel.

Being accurate

Don't rely on your memory when writing your novel. Always check your facts – preferably from several sources. If you make mistakes, you will lose credibility and disappoint your readers.

Using the experts

Don't be afraid to talk to people who are experts in their fields. You will learn details that you might not find in books. These touches will give your novel authenticity.

Producing the historical novel

This type of novel probably requires more research than any other. Dates, costume, events and way of life must be accurate if you are to create a believable story. If you introduce real historical figures, don't make them attend functions in London if they were actually in Bristol at the time. Check their whereabouts to see if they could have attended a particular ball or celebration.

Ensure that the costume, food and way of life is as accurate as you can make it. The further back in time you go, the more difficult it will be to find accurate details about the way of life.

Experimenting with science fiction

Science fiction writers have to use their imagination but even here, there must be some basis of truth. Start with the germ of an idea. What if...? Continue from there and see where it leads you, but talk to scientists and technologists to ensure that your ideas are not so improbable that your reader will scoff at them. They have to be believable in their terms.

Liverpool University Library houses the Science Fiction Foundation Research Library and this may be of use to the would-be science fiction writer. It is advisable to make an appointment to visit. The address is: PO Box 123, Liverpool L69 3DA. Tel: (0151) 794 2733/2696.

Creating real characters

Novels will only be successful if their characters are believable. Situations and the problems people face may change over the years but the people themselves don't change. Your biggest research aid for your characters is people. Never lose the opportunity to meet new individuals. Make notes on eccentric characters; jot down an unusual costume worn by a teenager; eavesdrop on other people's conversation; as soon as you can, write down any 'gems' you hear. Listen to the way in which people from different classes and jobs talk. While you cannot reproduce actual dialogue, it must be based on what you hear every day.

You can't use real people in your novel but incorporate different characteristics from various people to produce a composite character.

Contacting a publisher

When you have written your novel, study the *Writers' and Artists' Year Book* or the *Writers' Handbook* to see which publishers publish the type of novel you have written. Don't send a novel to a publisher who only publishes non-fiction! Browse in your local bookshops to see what publishers are currently publishing and see where your work will fit in.

When you have identified several publishers, send a query letter to each of them. Don't forget to send a stamped addressed envelope. Give a brief outline of the book and ask if they would be interested in seeing a synopsis and sample chapters.

If you are very confident, you could try to get a contract before you complete the novel. Established authors usually do this but if you are a beginner, it is unlikely any publisher will give a contract to an unknown writer before seeing the whole manuscript.

Revising the points

- Choose your own way of research.

- Be accurate.

- Create real characters.

PLANNING YOUR NON-FICTION WORK

When planning a non-fiction book, it is advisable to get a contract before you do most of the writing.

Writing query letters

Write a query letter giving brief details of the work you plan and ask if the editor is interested in an article or book on that subject. With the advent of word processors, it is easy to send several letters to different editors at the same time. The advantage of getting editors interested at an early stage is that you don't waste your time writing something they don't want. By writing to several editors simultaneously, you save time and you may get several favourable replies.

Changing direction

Sometimes your research may lead you in a different direction from the one in which you had planned to go. If you have already written a synopsis on the basis of which you have signed a contract, you will have to contact your editor to check that your new direction is acceptable. If you are writing a novel and have no contract yet, you are, of course, free to change whatever you like.

WRITING YOUR ARTICLE

Researching your market

Before starting on your article, do study the magazines for which you hope to write. Check that they contain your type of article and note the style and length of the work.

Writing to editors

Write a number of query letters to the editors of the magazines you have chosen. Check the name of the features editor. It is always advisable to send a letter to a person rather than a 'position'. Give a brief outline of your prospective article asking if the editor is interested and asking how many words are required. If you can also provide photographs, say so.

You may be invited to send the manuscript in 'on speculation'. This means the editor wishes to see the finished work before it is commissioned. Most articles submitted in this way are accepted but not all. Do keep to the number of words the editor asks for.

If several magazines express an interest, you can use the same information but write it with a different slant and in a different style. Do make sure your style is appropriate for the magazine you are writing for.

Gathering background information

You will usually need to research more background information than you can put into your article. When you come to write the article, you have a variety of facts and incidents from which to select your final material.

Using photographs

Photographs will often sell an article, so take a number from which you can select. Remember that you should obtain permission if you wish to include a picture of a person or an item that has a personal owner. There is more information about photographs in Chapter 8.

Checking details

Always make sure your facts are accurate and you have made the article as interesting as possible. The unusual or the different will make your article stand out. Search out unusual facts or incidents. You might be able to write a whole article around them.

WORKING ON YOUR BIOGRAPHY

If you want to write a biography, check that there has not been a recent one of your subject. If one was written thirty years or more earlier, you are probably safe to suggest it. Facts and dates are extremely important. Check several sources for information; don't rely on one.

Contacting a publisher

Before you start work on it, write to several publishers to ask if they are interested. If none of them is, you may need to think of another subject.

Obtaining permission

Although unofficial biographies are written, if your subject is still alive, it is courteous to ask if he or she is willing for you to attempt the work. If the subject has died recently, you may need to obtain permission from the relatives or the estate. For an older biography this is not necessary but do check that one has not been written recently.

Selecting material

You will gather far more information than you will be able to use so select your material carefully. Your subject should come to life on your pages. In a popular biography, dialogue is acceptable and this helps the characterisation. If there are letters and diaries available, try to use the actual words the subject would have spoken. You may have to adapt them but you can produce the 'flavour' of the time if it is not contemporary.

WRITING A TEXTBOOK

Finding a gap in the market

Textbooks are usually commissioned by publishers. Sometimes they will advertise for writers to contribute to a particular series. Browse through the education section of your local bookshops and see what is on offer. Even more importantly see what is *not* there. Look at the list of books in the series and see if there is a title you could contribute that is missing.

Write to the series editor to suggest it. Don't start the work until you have a publisher's interest *and* a contract.

Acknowledging your sources
Don't forget to keep a record of your sources so you can acknowledge them in your book.

Filing your information
Have an orderly filing system so that you can easily find the material you used and watch for any articles or new books on your subject.

Updating your work
Textbooks often become out of date. This is perhaps truer in certain subjects than others. The publishers may require you to update your material. You must be prepared to do this so it is essential that you keep up to date with current trends in your subject.

WRITING FOR CHILDREN

This branch of writing needs as much research as any other. Facts still have to be accurate and presented in a readable way.

Avoiding the pitfalls
Don't fall into the trap of thinking writing for children is an easy option. It isn't! Children are not fools and don't like to be patronised. They are individuals and like to be treated as such. Your research must be thorough if you are writing a non-fiction book or an historical novel and it is a good idea to read a number of children's books of the type you hope to write. If you are writing for five-year-olds, your style will obviously be different from that of a teenage novel.

Minding your language
Be careful with your language. Don't use words which are so simple, the child is bored. Children like to be challenged so don't be afraid of using some more difficult words. But don't include too many or the work will be incomprehensible for any but the infant prodigy!

Remember that language is changing all the time. This is particularly true of slang words used by the young. The only way to get your language accurate is to mix with young people and listen to them. But avoid using too many current 'in' words unless you wish your work to be so dated it cannot be reprinted later.

REVISING THE POINTS

- Research the market.
- Write query letters.
- Be aware of changing direction.
- Find a gap in the market.

CASE STUDIES

Esther collates her material

Esther has already been commissioned by *Surrey County Magazine* to write the article 'Shere Delight' and she is now in a position to put together her notes and decide which photographs she will use. She starts to write the article.

Andrew writes a query letter

Andrew has nearly finished his novel and decides that he will write to some publishers. He writes the query letter in Figure 9.

Dear Miss Harris

I am in the process of writing a novel set during the Second World War. The hero, Ralph, is a Battle of Britain pilot. His parents own a pub in Coventry which is bombed. They are both killed and Ralph becomes very bitter. He doesn't get on with his colleagues as his background is so different from theirs. He falls in love with a Wing Commander's daughter. Her father does not approve and they have a stormy relationship.

Would you be interested in seeing a detailed synopsis and some sample chapters?

I enclose an SAE for your convenience.

Yours sincerely

Andrew Brown

Fig. 9. Andrew's query letter to a publisher.

Molly continues to write

Molly has already received a contract from a publisher to write the book on the suffragettes and she is more than halfway through it when she realises she has deviated from the original synopsis sent to her editor. She makes detailed notes about the changes and rings the editor. Fortunately there is no problem and Molly is told to continue her work. But she is asked to submit a new synopsis for the perusal of the editor.

11

Producing the Finished Work

Now that you have done all your research and sorted out your notes, it is time to put the work together. You have probably already written some of it. The research and planning stages always take far longer than the actual writing.

COLLATING THE MATERIAL

Go through all the notes you have made and listen to any tapes. Discard any material that you will not be using and if you have not already done so, organise the material you have selected in the order in which you will use it. Sometimes it is helpful to write headlines for yourself and delete them as you write up the work.

WRITING THE PIECE

This is the best bit. At last you are actually writing and using the research you have done. The length of time it takes you to write will, of course, depend on what you are writing. If it is non-fiction, make sure that by this stage you have found a publisher for your work.

If you are writing a novel, now is the time to do more market research to discover which publishers might be interested in looking at your work. You may be able to send off a synopsis and some sample chapters.

EDITING THE MATERIAL

Editing your work is vitally important. You will probably not be satisfied with your first draft and much rewriting may be needed. Go through it a number of times before it is ready for submission. It is often a good idea to leave it for a day or two and come back to check it later. Do make sure the finished product is as good as you can make it. Don't leave any unnecessary mistakes. Spell checks on word processors are a great help. It's so easy to make typing errors if you are trying to work quickly. But do check your work as well. The spell check will only correct spelling mistakes. It won't be able to read your mind and point out incorrect words. If you've typed 'he' instead of 'the', it will stay until you correct it.

SUBMITTING YOUR WORK

You have done your market research and the editor to whom you have written has expressed an interest. Make sure you present your material in the correct way. The title pages should contain the title of the piece and the number of words. Put your name underneath and your address in the bottom right-hand corner.

Use double spacing and type on one side of A4 paper only. Use good quality paper and number the pages. For short pieces use paper clips for fastening – not staples. Bind longer pieces together with a rubber band; don't put the work in a folder.

Don't forget to enclose return postage or an addressed envelope with the right number of stamps. Always enclose a covering letter with the work.

REVISING THE POINTS

- Edit your work carefully.
- Write on one side of A4 paper only.
- Use double spacing.
- Send a covering letter.
- Enclose an SAE or return postage.

CASE STUDIES

Esther sends off her article

Esther has completed her article, numbered the pages and done a title page. Before putting the transparencies into the A4 plastic envelopes designed for this purpose, she labels them and numbers them. She also types out a list of the twelve slides she has enclosed. The editor will choose the ones she needs. With the article Esther

SHERE DELIGHT
One of Surrey's prettiest villages has a great deal more to it than meets the immediate eye

In 1086 the Manor of Shere, near Guildford, was worth fifteen pounds! It was given by William the Conqueror to the Earl of Surrey, having been in Royal Possession since the time of Edward the Confessor whose wife 'Eddit (Edith), the Queen, did hold it'.

The Manor, the central estate which received the tenant's dues, appears in the Domesday Book where it was 'rated for nine hides'. A hide, one hundred and twenty acres, was the amount of land considered necessary to support a peasant family for a year. The Manor also boasted fourteen ploughs, each consisting of eight oxen which formed a team; two of these were used solely to produce profit for the Lord whose Hall was situated in the Manor.

Over the next two centuries the Manor changed hands several times and in 1461 Lord Audley received it from Edward IV. This Lord of the Manor is buried beneath a brass memorial tablet in St James Church. But there is no memorial for his son, James, who led the rebels against Henry VII in the Cornish rebellion of 1497. He marched through Shere to Blackheath, where he was soundly defeated by the King's army, and he ended his life on the scaffold. The Manor of Shere, 'having thereby escheated to the Crown', was then given by the King to Sir Reginald Bray, in whose family it has remained ever since.

The present Lord of the Manor is the first lady to hold the title. Mrs Handa Bray inherited the Manor of Shere from her grandfather in February 1964 and has lived since 1976 in High House. Her main role is still that of a landlord – a difficult one today when estates are so expensive to maintain. When capital was needed, she decided to keep most of the cottages 'because they are most necessary to Shere'; and sell all but one of the outlying farms. Old methods of farming are still used on this and the tenant's family has farmed in Shere for several generations.

Fig. 10. Published article 'Shere Delight'.

The link with the past is very strong. Some of the cottages have been sold to outsiders but they are not permitted to alter the outward appearance of the historic buildings, although the interiors may be modernised. However, many are still inhabited by descendants of the original families.

One of the houses in the main street still retains the remains of an early fifteenth-century building and is probably the oldest one in the village. An interesting early artefact was also found recently. When the wall of one of the cottages was being repaired, an old brown felt hat was discovered. It was identified as one from the Tudor period and, the London Museum having done some excellent renovation work, the restored headgear how resides in the small museum in the village. How it arrived in its hiding place is a mystery, but fortunately there is no evidence that its owner was attached to it at the time!

During the seventeenth century a number of the cottages were sold, but during the following century William Bray, a solicitor, determined to redeem the family fortunes and bought many of them back. A redoubtable gentleman, William did not believe in wasting time or talent. When the man who had started the monumental History of Surrey died in 1802, William was determined to complete it and in his enthusiasm he visited every parish in the county making detailed notes. He finally achieved his aim when the last volume was published in 1814.

At different times he lived in several of the cottages he had bought and finally died in 1832 at the age of ninety-six in Old Manor Cottages, a sixteenth-century open hall house. This he bequeathed to his daugther, Catherine, who remained in it until her death in 1854. William is commemorated by a tablet in St James Church and was highly esteemed by the parishioners who paid tribute to his 'zeal and ability rarely excelled'.

In the Domesday Book there is a record of a church at 'Essira' (Shere) in 1087 and it is likely there was a Saxon church on the site as early as the seventh century. However, the present building dates from

Fig. 10. Contd.

the end of the twelfth century and a board lists the Rectors 'as known' from 1270 to the last induction in 1989. The unbroken line from Ilarius in 1270 to the present incumbent is a witness to the enduring faith of the village throughout the centuries.

In the chancel can be found a fourteenth-century quatrefoil and squint through which Christine Carpenter, the Anchoress of Shere, was able to receive communion and see the altar. Outside the church, on the north wall, a small plaque is the only remaining evidence of the cell where she was incarcerated by her own wish in 1329. But her story does not end there. After three years in her prison she escaped, but in a short while she repented of the sin of breaking her vows and was 'thrust back into the said re-enclosure'. The Bishop ordered her to be closely guarded so she realised 'how nefarious was her committed sin'. It is not known how long she remained there before she died.

The church has other interesting connections. In 1551 Margaret Roper, the granddaughter of Sir Thomas More, was married there.

Her sister, Elizabeth, had a son Reynolde, who was baptised in Shere in 1555. Yet another thread was woven into the past when the father of the present Lord of the Manor was also christened Reynolde. He was a member of the British Canadian Arctic Expedition and sadly he was drowned in the Arctic soon after Mrs Handa Bray was born, so never took on his role.

The patronage of the living of St James was granted to the Brays, as Lords of the Manor, in the sixteenth century. The Duncombe family provided the Rectors from 1658 until 1843, nearly two hundred years – a remarkable record. In 1676 Edward Bray sold the patronage of the living to the then current Rector, Thomas Duncombe, who served in this capacity for fifty-six years! When the Duncombes left the village in the nineteenth century, the patronage of the living reverted to the Brays, who still retain it. In the Bray Chapel bordering the Lady Chapel are many memorials to the family. Also much in evidence is their crest, the Hemp Bray, a machine used for breaking flax.

Fig. 10. Contd.

Two other interesting links with the past can be found on the south side of the church. In a glass case is a minute fourteenth-century Madonna and Child, probably lost from the staff of a pilgrim making his pilgrimage along the Pilgrim's Way to Canterbury. Opposite this, from the same century, is an oak Crusader Alms coffer, one of many placed in parish churches by Pope Innocent III. Gifts placed in the coffer were for the support of the Crusaders in their Holy War.

Shere was not without its characters. One of these was William Hicks, born in 1780, into a wealthy Surrey family. Disappointed in love, he became mentally unstable and deterioriated into a tramp, living in squalor. After his parents died, he reverted to the role of country gentleman but he took to gambling and his behaviour was still unstable. In 1820, while attending a race meeting at Ascot, he threw his hat at the King, who was not amused. 'Billy' never saw his hat again, a fact which he apparently resented more than the nine months' prison sentence he received for this offence!

The Misses Spottiswood who lived later in the nineteenth century would no doubt have disapproved thoroughly of William and his lifestyle. They abhorred alcohol, which they considered a production of the devil, and felt that an alternative drink – water – should be provided for the villagers. Accordingly they ordered a well to be dug in 1886. Their initials are entwined on a brass plaque above the well which remained in use until the 1970s when the Thames Water Board stopped the spring by sinking fresh bore holes. Whether the villages actually forsook real ale for Adam's ale is not recorded!

However frequently one visits it, there is always something fresh to discover in this beautiful medieval village set on the banks of the Tillingbourne and visitors constantly agree the village is a 'Shere Delight'.

Fig. 10. Contd.

encloses a covering letter and an SAE for the return of the photographs. She does not need to send return postage for the article as it has been commissioned. For the completed article, see Figure 10.

Andrew sends off a synopsis and sample chapter

Andrew has had a reply to one of his query letters and to his delight, the editor invites him to send a synopsis and the first chapter. He edits his synopsis and spends a lot of time editing and changing his first chapter. He fastens the pages together with paper clips and writes a covering letter (see Figure 11).

Dear Ms Smith

Thank you for your letter inviting me to submit a synopsis and the first chapter of my novel, 'Never Say Die'. I now enclose these and also postage for their return should the novel not prove suitable for your list.

Yours sincerely

Andrew Brown

Fig. 11. Andrew's covering letter to an editor.

Molly sends off her work

Molly has completed and edited her account of the suffragettes. She numbers the pages, does a title page (see Figure 12) and binds the papers together with a rubber band. She writes a covering letter and posts the work off to her publisher. She does not include return postage as the work has been commissioned.

A MONSTROUS REGIMENT OF WOMEN
(An account of the suffragette movement)
(Approx. 75,000 words)

MOLLY GREY

22 Crowther Close
Bedford
BD2 8AB

Fig. 12. Molly's title page.

Glossary

Anachronism. Referring to an event, custom or item in the wrong period.

Anchoress. A woman who chose to be enclosed alone in a small cell so she could pray and meditate with no distractions.

Archives. Historical records which have been preserved.

Bookmarking. Adding an address to your on-line address book.

Browser. A tool which enables you to move from one web page to another.

Commission. To contract a writer to produce a particular piece of work.

Contract. A written agreement to produce a particular piece of work by a certain time. It is signed by the publisher and the author.

Covering letter. A letter sent with a manuscript.

Database. Lists of data stored in electronic form.

Download. To transfer material from one computer to another.

Editing. Checking and correcting work.

Editor. The person who commissions work from a writer on behalf of a publisher or magazine. The editor also works with the writer to produce the final material.

Email. Electronic mail. Messages sent from one computer to another.

Home page. The first page of a web site.

Internet. A network of computers which are linked around the world by phone lines.

Internet service provider. A company from which you can buy access to the internet.

Microfiches. Small plastic sheets containing lists which are magnified when inserted into a machine.

Modem. The attachment that will link your computer to the telephone line so that you can have access to the internet.

Newsgroups. Electronic noticeboard used on the internet.

On spec. Sending work to an editor hoping it may be accepted but with no guarantee.

Primary sources. Diaries, letters and other material providing first-hand information.

Query letter. Letter written to an editor outlining a proposed piece of work and asking if the publisher or magazine would be interested.

Quatrefoil. A small hole shaped like a four-leafed clover sometimes found in the wall of a church.

Secondary sources. Material produced after the event as a result of researching primary sources.

Squint. Small hole through which the viewer can see but not be seen.

Surfing. Looking around the Internet.

Web page. Part of a web site.

Web site. A collection of web pages.

World wide web. Part of the Internet that consists of a vast collection of documents stored on computers all over the world.

Useful Reference Books

A History of Everyday Things in England, four volumes, B. T. Batsford Ltd.

A Punch History of Manners 1841–1940, A. Adburgham, Hutchinson.

Aslib Directory of Information Sources in the United Kingdom.

Food and Cooking in Britain, five booklets, English Heritage.

Getting Started on the Internet, Irene Krechowiecka, How To Books.

How They Lived, Asa Briggs, Blackwell.

National Trust Book of Christmas and Festive Day Recipes, Sara Paston-Williams.

Not in Front of the Servants, Frank Victor Dawes, National Trust Classics.

Research for Writers, Ann Hoffman, A. & C. Black.

Researching a Novel, Jean Saunders, Allison & Busby.

Speeches from the Classics, London Academy of Music and Dramatic Art.

The Internet for Writers, Nick Daws, Internet Handbooks.

The London Diplomatic List, HMSO.

The New Fowler's Modern English Usage, ed, R. W. Burchfield, Oxford University Press.

The New Shell Book of Firsts, Patrick Robertson, Headline.

The Polite World, J. Wildeblood and P. Brinson, Oxford University Press.

Using the Internet, Dorling Kindersley.

With Passport and Parasol, BBC.

World Cruising Handbook, A. & C. Black.

Useful Addresses

Alan Sutton Publishers Ltd, Phoenix Mill, Far Thrupp, Stroud, Gloucester GL5 2BU. Tel: (01453) 731114.

British Association of Picture Libraries and Agencies, 18 Vine Hill, London EC1R 5DX. Tel: (020) 7713 1780.

British Film Institute Library, 21 Stephen Street, London W1P 1PL. Tel: (020) 7255 1444.

British Library, St Pancras, 96 Euston Road, London NW1 2DB. Tel: Switchboard: (020) 7412 7000; Manuscript Office: (020) 7412 7513; Reader Admissions Office: (020) 7412 7513; Visitors' Services: (020) 7412 7332.

General Register Office, St Catherine's House, 10 Kingsway, London WC2B 6JP. Tel: (020) 7242 0262.

Hamilton House Mailings Ltd, 17 Staveley Way, Brixworth Industrial Park, Northampton NN6 9TX. Tel: (01604) 881889.

Kentwell Hall Historical Re-Creations, Long Milford, Suffolk CO10 9BA. Tel: (01787) 310207.

London Academy of Music and Dramatic Art, Tower House, 226 Cromwell Road, London SW5 0SR. Tel: (020) 7373 4337.

London Transport Museum, Covent Garden, London. Tel: (020) 7379 6344.

National Register of Archives, Quality House, Quality Court, Chancery Lane, London WC2A 1HP.

National Sound Archive (British Library), 29 Exhibition Road, South Kensington, London SW7 2AS. Tel: (020) 7589 6603.

Public Record Office, Ruskin Avenue, Kew, Richmond, Surrey TW9 4DU. Tel: (020) 8876 3444.

Public Record Office of Northern Ireland, 66 Balmoral Avenue, Belfast BT9 6NY. Tel: (028) 9025 1318.

Science Fiction Foundation Research Library, PO Box 123, Liverpool L69 3DA. Tel: (0151) 794 2733/2696.

Scottish Record Office, HM General Register House, Edinburgh EH1 3YY. Tel: (0131) 566 6585.

Internet Cafés

Carlisle Business Centre, 60 Carlisle Road, Carlisle. Tel: (01274) 223300.

Cybercafé, 2–3 Phoenix Court, Guildford GU1 3EG. Tel: (01483) 451945.

Cybercafé, 76 Boundary Road, Walthamstow E17. Tel: (020) 8509 0944.

Cyberia, 39 Whitfield Street, London. Tel: (020) 7681 4200.

Cybernet Café, Margaret Street, London.

Punters Cybercafé, 111 Arundel Street, Sheffield. Tel: (0114) 276 2668.

The Arcadian Centre, Hunt Street, Birmingham. Tel: (0121) 622 4010.

Index